Breaking Down the Walls... and the Gospel

The Subversive Work of "Evangelical Inclusivism"

BREAKING
DOWN
THE WALLS . . .
and the GOSPEL

The Subversive Work
of "Evangelical Inclusivism"

Raymond L. Teachout

2650 MONT-JOLI, STE-FOY, QUÉBEC, GIV IC6 CANADA - info@ebpa-publications.org

Breaking Down the Walls . . . and the Gospel:
The Subversive Work of "Evangelical Inclusivism"

Copyright © 1999 by Raymond L. Teachout

Published by:
  Études Bibliques pour Aujourd'hui (*Bible Studies for Today*)
  2650 Mont-Joli, Ste-Foy, PQ G1V-1C6 Canada
  info@ebpa-publications.org www.ebpa-publications.org

Printed in Canada   3rd printing

ISBN 2-9804339-4-2

Legal deposit: National Library of Canada
                  Bibliothèque nationale du Québec

Distributed in the USA by:
  Dr. Lance T. Ketchum
  Executive Secretary
  Minnesota Baptist Association
  5000 Golden Valley Road
  Golden Valley, MN 55422
  (763) 588-2755

DEDICATION

This book is dedicated to Dr. Michael Windsor, whose life and teaching were exemplary to me while in seminary. It was in the context of his courses that I began my research on evangelical inclusivism.

ACKNOWLEDGMENTS

This book has been the fruit of many people's labor. I am grateful to God for the invaluable help I have received along the way from many people. Special thanks to Adam Blumer, Melinda Clark, Jennifer Durrand (who is now my precious wife), Walter Loescher, John P. Shay, and my parents, who have sacrificed much of their time to see this project completed.

TABLE OF CONTENTS

FOREWORD

T HIS BOOK is small in size, but big in importance. The information it contains is vital for all Christians who are willing to learn the truth about the cost American Christianity has paid because of its toleration and espousal of the philosophy of inclusivism.

Raymond L. Teachout, the author, is completely qualified to write such a study. He is intelligent, he is informed, he has been well-trained, and he is a younger member of a family that has distinguished itself both in the service of Jesus Christ, and in the defense of the faith "once, for all, committed to the saints" (Jude 3).

When my wife and I arrived in French Equatorial Africa, in 1955, Raymond's grandparents, Dick and Oril Teachout, were senior missionaries on that field. At great sacrifice, they had labored until an area once totally unreached with the Gospel had come to have hundreds of Christians and a host of village churches. Dick, Sr, was an uncompromising fundamentalist, gracious and loving, but fully dedicated to the Word of God.

Raymond Teachout's father and mother, Richard, Jr., and Nancy Teachout, were also missionaries to that same area - now called the Central African Republic. Later, they served as church-planters in France, and are now "senior missionaries" in Quebec. Dick, Jr., has written books and articles, both in French and in English, in the defense of Biblical Christianity.

By virtue of such a heritage, Raymond L Teachout knows the difference between a genuine, pure, and knowledgeable faith in Christ and the Word of God, and the pseudo Christianity so often embraced and expounded in Twentieth-Century America.   In this book, he makes it possible for his reader to know the difference.

Victories won for the Christ of the Bible and for the Bible itself will not be final and complete until our Lord returns. Until that glorious day, it is essential that young men continue to do the intensive study and write the books that will help us not to trade Bible truth for "a mess of potage." My friend and former student, Raymond L Teachout is obviously one of those young men.

C. Raymond Buck, PhD
—————————————
President-Emeritus, Baptist Mid-Missions
Chairman, Department of Missions and Evangelism
at Central Baptist Theological Seminary of Minneapolis

INTRODUCTION

"WHAT'S THE MATTER?" asked Francine as her perplexed son plopped himself onto a living room couch.

"It's just . . . I don't know what to think anymore."

"About what?"

"About salvation, the gospel . . . about the truth in general."

Francine thought for a moment. Then she came and sat down next to her teenage son.

"Can you explain what you mean, Michael?"

"Well, today at school, in Bible class, Mr. Johnston got into this lecture about pride and those that think that they are always right. He went on to talk about our religious opinions and beliefs, and said that no matter how much we might be convinced about something from the Bible, we have to be humble and admit that our beliefs are only that—they're only our opinions, views and interpretations. Our views may certainly be right, he said, but in the mean time, we shouldn't be as dogmatic as are some in our circles. He went on to say that even what we, as a Christian church and school, believe about salvation should not make us look down on others in broad Christendom who understand salvation differently than us. He said, 'Who are we anyway to say that other devout and pious people are not saved?' You know Mom, that's what I don't understand. If we really believed that salvation is one way, how can we say that those who are going another way are saved? I don't get it, Mom."

"Oh son," replied Francine tenderly, "you worry too much about those things. You know your teacher has much experience in the Word of God. Why don't you trust him in this matter? Better yet, trust God. Think of it! You wouldn't want to play God, and act as if you knew it all, would you? I know *I* would not want to be the judge to decide who will go to heaven or not. That would be presumptuous! I'll let God determine that one. I think that's what your teacher was trying to say. . . ."

Far-fetched? Unthinkable? Not in 20th century evangelical Christianity. Other eras of church history were often characterized by dogmatic thinking and heresy hunts, but this century has seen the tide reversed as relativism has made great inroads into Christendom.

This relativism has come in a dangerous form, that of inclusivism. Inclusivism is not easy to detect because it is often mistaken for a kind spirit of tolerance. Furthermore, it is hard to detect because it comes with an affirmation of what inclusivism believes is truth, coupled with an approval of what it believes is error. There have been inclusive liberals who seek conciliation with those of opposing beliefs, and there have been inclusive Catholics, who appeal for Christian fellowship with professing believers outside the Church. With this relativistic inclusivism, anyone can "strongly" hold to his beliefs while giving credence to opposing view points.

This inroad of relativism into Christendom has not stopped at the door of those who profess the biblical gospel. Even within the evangelical arena, there has been a substantial penetration of relativism . . . the relativism of inclusivism. True, there is probably no evangelical who will admit a belief in relativism. However, there are some who will proclaim the evangelical gospel, yet argue that others within Christendom are saved, even though they hold opposing view-points on the gospel. This then is an evangelical type of inclusivism that legitimizes what were once considered false gospels, and embraces as brethren those who were once considered apostate.[1]

How has this belief crept into the community of saints? What has made inclusivism acceptable to a growing number of evangelicals? In Part One, I will attempt to answer many such questions by tracing the major developments of inclusivism in this past century. The early part of the century saw inclusivism at work in the downfall of mainline Protestant denominations. We will consider, in Chapter One, some of the events which took place in the Northern Baptist Convention and the Presbyterian Church. Following that time, another major outworking of inclusivism began. This was seen in the influential leadership of Billy Graham. The second chapter focuses on outlining Graham's inclusive beliefs as they developed over the decades. The final chapter of Part One looks at some current trends and contemporary developments involving some key evangelical leaders and movements.

What is the answer to the problem of evangelical inclusivism? Very simply, it is a firm biblical allegiance to the gospel, coupled with a sound, biblical approach to truth. We will consider these matters in Part Two. As we will learn, evangelical inclusivists often do not err explicitly in their view of the gospel. Instead they err in how they approach the truths of the gospel. Sadly, they approach the evangelical gospel—to which they hold—no longer as absolute *truth* but as personal *opinion* only.

Therefore, while my concern is for the integrity of the biblical gospel, this book does not address in great detail all the questions surrounding the gospel and salvation. It does not claim to be a theological treatise on soteriology (the doctrine of salvation), but the final chapter will touch on this subject. More importantly, throughout the book, we will focus on issues of *consistency* in how one approaches the concept of truth. My goal will be to show that in legitimizing false gospels, an inclusive gospel is subtly, yet distinctly, opposed to the biblical gospel. It thus results in subverting, corrupting and ultimately repudiating the very gospel it claims to endorse. Therefore, this "evangelical" inclusive gospel should be thoroughly rejected as a different, and therefore false gospel (see Gal. 1).

I also want to add that "evangelical inclusivism" is technically a contradiction in terms, since the *"evangel"* (the gospel), is by definition NOT inclusive! Thus, in reality, there is nothing truly evangelical in inclusivism! Yet I believe the term *evangelical inclusivism* is relevant and appropriate for two reasons. First, because the term limits our consideration of inclusivism to that which concerns the *"evangel"* (the gospel). I am not saying that issues regarding other doctrines are not important. They are! However, if our gospel is unclear and lost, then we have nothing more to preach. Therefore, I have purposefully limited my topic to the gospel, and how inclusivism affects it.

Second, the term *evangelical inclusivism* is relevant because it conveys a certain inclusivism that can only occur within evangelicalism. A liberal can hold to inclusivism, a Catholic can hold to inclusivism, but neither can hold to "evangelical inclusivism" since neither are professed evangelicals. By very definition, therefore, only professing evangelicals[2] can embrace *evangelical inclusivism*. I am not concerned for the inclusivism that takes place within liberalism or Catholicism—because they do not even have the gospel—but I am concerned about its growing presence within the evangelical community. Thus, the term *evangelical inclusivism* communicates a problem and a poison that is *within* the ranks of those who profess the biblical gospel. Because of this, the problem is all the more urgent and critical![3]

This book is not on separation. Your first reaction might have been to expect otherwise, considering the focus on inclusivism. However, biblical separation concerns born-again believers. The Scriptural injunctions to "come out from among them, and be ye separate" (2 Cor. 6:17), and to "withdraw from every brother that walks disorderly" (2 Thess. 3:6 NKJV) were given to God's children, not to lost people. Before dealing with issues of separation, the subject of the gospel must be brought into focus, especially in times when the gospel message is muddled.

The point is this: I am not talking about a Christian who collaborates with someone whom he knows is not saved. The issue involved in such a case is separation. I am talking about a professing evangelical who collaborates with someone he believes is a Christian though that person has contrary beliefs concerning salvation. In such a case, the problem is with the professing evangelical's understanding of the gospel.

Too many Christians naturally assume that the gospel is never at stake whenever and wherever the *evangelical* name is claimed. They take for granted that an "evangelical" is someone who is saved. Some Christians might invoke problems of separation and compromise with evangelicals who fellowship with the perceived enemy, yet they rarely put into question the validity of such evangelicals' professed faith. They overlook the possibility that the problem may lie precisely in the content of the professed faith. It is absolutely essential that our Christian discernment functions on the basis of a clear understanding of the gospel of Jesus Christ. Therefore, regarding inclusive evangelicals, it is first necessary to examine whether or not their inclusive gospel is the valid and true gospel. In this book, I will attempt to demonstrate that the evangelical inclusive gospel is opposed to the true gospel. Therefore, those who hold conscientiously to an inclusive gospel are in greater need of a sound presentation of the unadulterated gospel than a call to biblical separation.

In considering this subject, I would like to be cautious in the way I treat the issues and the men behind the issues. Just as Peter and Barnabas strayed away from the purity of the gospel momentarily (Gal. 2:11-16), it is possible for true believers—even those who hold influential positions—to be swayed momentarily by false apostles. These deceived believers are different from those entrenched in their inclusive-gospel beliefs. These last preach another gospel and have God's "anathema" upon them (Gal. 1). While it is possible and biblically necessary to repudiate a false belief system, it is impossible to see the heart of individuals who do profess an evangelical faith. Therefore, I have not sought to necessarily categorize those whom I have mentioned in this book as either entrenched inclusivists or momentarily deceived believers (time will reveal that). The point is not to make strict lists of who is what, but to repudiate the inclusive gospel that is appealing to so many, and to warn those who are embracing it as to the error of their way.

There may be believers who are inclusive by ignorance rather than by conviction. Some Christians may be influenced by inclusive evangelicals into thinking that those once considered apostates are truly "brothers and sisters" in Christ though of a different tradition. This they might accept, not necessarily because they endorse inclusivism, but because they are ignorant of what these "brethren" really teach on the gospel. While ignorance is never an excuse, the root of the problem is with those who are knowledgeable, and yet are firmly inclusive by conviction. Therefore, let the ignorant gain wisdom and let evangelical inclusivism be exposed for what it truly is: a wolf in sheep's clothing.

NOTES ON THE INTRODUCTION

1. I use the term apostate to speak either of those who have fallen away from their professed faith, or of those who are in organizations or denominations that no longer proclaim the true gospel. I understand that there may be genuine believers who have not yet come out of apostate organizations; I am not speaking of such people, since, by virtue of their beliefs, they do not truly belong in the organization or denomination of which they are a part.

2. When speaking of evangelicals, I am referring to those who profess the traditionally understood evangelical gospel. I am not necessarily speaking of those who in the contemporary movement are known by the term "evangelical." Thus the term is encountered at times before the contemporary evangelical movement began (1940s; then called New-evangelical). However, in the second and third chapter of this book, the trends discussed will most often be those occurring in the mainline evangelical movement.

3. My use of the term "inclusivism" is in harmony with the use some have made of it in the context of the liberal-fundamentalist controversy. It is, however, wider in scope than the current use of the term in contemporary theological circles. Today, the terms inclusivism and exclusivism are used mostly (if not always) in relation to the issue of whether or not salvation can be attained by those who have never heard the gospel (that specific issue will be addressed briefly in the third and fifth chapters of the book). My use of the term includes but is not restricted to its specific current use: inclusivism will be shown to deal not only with those who have never heard the gospel, but also with those who have embraced a false type of Christianity.

Part 1

THE DEVELOPMENT OF EVANGELICAL INCLUSIVISM IN THE 20TH CENTURY

Chapter I

THE FALLING OF THE GIANTS
-- A LOOK AT THE LIBERAL/FUNDAMENTAL CONTROVERSY

A fundamentalist who accepts the concept of an inclusive church ceases to be a fundamentalist. Conservatives and liberals might regard orthodox Biblical theology as one of the forms of faith recognized in the church, but fundamentalists insist it is the faith of the church. . . . — Oliver Price [1]

FINDING ITS ORIGINS in German higher critical thinking, liberalism crept into the Protestant scene of North America toward the end of the 19th century. Battles were fought—and lost—over its acceptance within the Protestant denominations. The battles were particularly fierce in the Northern Baptist Convention and the Presbyterian Church.[2] Therefore, the matter of inclusivism will be considered mostly in connection with these two denominations. Beyond any other issue, it was the matter regarding inclusivism that determined the outcome of the denominational controversies. We today need to learn from these lessons of history.

THREE IDEOLOGICAL CAMPS

Regardless of denomination, three ideological camps spanned early 20th century Protestantism: fundamentalism, liberalism, and moderate conservatism.[3]

1. Fundamentalism

Those of the first camp, most often simply called the fundamentalists, formed the group that held most firmly to the orthodox faith given in Scriptures. They were also called by some "militants," "radicals," or "extreme fundamentalists."[4]   Of fundamentalism, Kirsopp Lake, an avowed liberal, said:

> It represents an unwavering attachment to the great traditional doctrines of Christianity. The name "Fundamentalist," was, I believe, first given to them some years ago when they adopted the "quadrilateral of belief," —the Infallible Inspiration of Scripture, the Deity of Jesus Christ, the efficacy of the Blood Atonement, and the Second Coming of the Lord. . . . But it is a mistake, often made by educated persons who happen to have little knowledge of historical theology, to suppose that Fundamentalism is a new and strange form of thought. It is nothing of the kind: it is the partial and uneducated survival of a theology which was once universally held by all Christians. . . . The Fundamentalist may be wrong; I think that he is. But it is we who have departed from the tradition, not he, and I am sorry for the fate of anyone who tries to argue with the Fundamentalist on the basis of authority. The Bible and the *corpus theologicum* of the Church is [sic] on the Fundamentalist side.[5]

2. Liberalism

There is difficulty in defining concisely what those of the second group believed. The liberals or modernists, denied supernaturalism[6] and believed in the evolutionary processes both of man and of religion. In their minds, they were continuing the Christian tradition, not in a static way, but in a "living" way. Liberals knew that their teaching came in great contrast to the faith of the fundamentalists. And they were not alone in understanding the differences. In his well known book, <u>Christianity and Liberalism</u>, Machen, a fundamentalist, argues at length that liberalism "is a totally diverse type of religious belief, which is only the more destructive of the Christian faith because it makes use of traditional Christian terminology."[7] He adds that in spite of the liberal use of traditional phraseology, liberalism "not only is a different religion from Christianity but belongs in a totally different class of religions."[8] Machen's desire was

> [to] show that the liberal attempt at reconciling Christianity with modern science has really relinquished everything distinctive of Christianity, so 'that what remains is in essentials only that same indefinite type of religious aspiration which was in the world before Christianity came upon the scene.[9]

Of course liberals did not agree with Machen's portrait of modernism. They saw themselves, not as deniers of the faith but rather as ones transforming, modernizing and improving the faith to which Christianity of old held. Kirsopp Lake described the liberals as ones who believe in and who submit to what he calls a "purpose of life."[10] For the liberal, the submission to this ethical ideal is the modern equivalent to the submission to God as seen in the Bible. The essence of this religious experience is the same, but the experience itself is not. "Religion requires men who will make the experiments, and record them faithfully and intelligibly, not those who repeat other people's formulae [sic], and force their results to agree with them."[11] The liberal appreciates "the beauty of the language of the past, even though he cannot make that language his own, for the **theory** of the past is not the same as his own."[12]

Liberals also reacted strongly against the fundamentalists' attempt to put them out of their churches. According to the liberals, the fundamentalists were wrong to require them to hold to the fundamentalists' "formulae." As Lake says, modernists "claim the right to continue in the churches, and feel that the claim of the Fundamentalist to exclude them is based on a radically wrong conception which has survived from an earlier age."[13]

3. *Moderate Conservatism*

Early on, only two groups divided the Protestant scene in North America: fundamentalists and liberals. At the clash of these two groups, a noticeable third group appeared from within early fundamentalism. Though many in this third camp both considered themselves to be, and called themselves, fundamentalists,[14] they were known generally as moderates. Though conservative in their theology, they lacked the militancy of the strict fundamentalists toward liberalism. In other words, there was a limit to their concern for doctrine; they would stop short of splitting their denomination over modernism. Kirsopp Lake called this third group the "Institutionalists." This was a group that formed "a mediating position" which endeavored " . . . to reduce to a minimum the amount of 'opinion' which must be accepted. . . . Its real interest is not in thought, but in the institution as such. . . . Its members usually endeavour to compensate for a concession in one direction by obstinate emphasis in another."[15]

Moderates also seemed to understand the issues that their denominations were facing with modernism. This is illustrated by moderate conservative Frank Goodchild, pastor and leader among the early fundamentalists in the Northern Baptist Convention. As an early fundamentalist, he wrote:

> The real difference between the contending parties in the churches today is that the fundamentalists accept as true the New Testament's statement of certain facts, and the liberals deny that they are facts, or else they so explain them away that the New Testament writers would no longer recognize them. The facts that modernists deny are the great facts of the New Testament. They deny that Jesus Christ was virgin-born, though the New Testament says he was. They deny that he fulfilled prophecy, and worked miracles, though the New Testament says he did. They deny that he died as the sinner's substitute, though the New Testament says he did. They deny that the body that was crucified came out of the grave alive, though the New Testament says it did. They deny that he visibly ascended into heaven, though the New Testament says he did. They deny that he will come back to the world, though Jesus Christ and all his apostles declared that he would. What the New Testament declares,

fundamentalists believe. Modernists do not. That is the real difference between the two parties in the churches to-day.[16]

All parties involved in the controversy seemed to reveal an understanding of the vital issues at hand.

THE WATCHWORDS OF INCLUSIVISM: "TOLERATION" AND "UNITY"

When the Northern Baptist Convention (NBC) was officially organized in 1907, it was already inclusive, with liberals entrenched in the leadership of the body.[17] However, it was not until the 1920s that the issues were drawn clearly enough that the fundamentalists attempted to forge a solution to the problem of liberalism. If the conservative majority was to purge the Convention of liberalism, it would have had to repudiate, by the same token, the inclusivism which went with the liberal presence. As time would prove, this inclusivism would be the determining factor in whether or not the fundamentalists would win over modernism in the Convention.

The liberals knew that the fundamentalists were working to rid the denominations of their influence, and they did not sit idle. Marsden reports on the controversy:

> In 1924 and 1925, however, the principal theaters of action were the large Baptist and Presbyterian denominations in the Northern United States, where liberalism was under such heavy assault that it could not even win by direct frontal attack. Mathews and others attempted to persuade the denominations that modernism was a legitimate and superior form of Christianity. A far more effective counterattack, however, was the appeal to the strong American tradition of tolerance. In most American churches this ideal, at least in theory, was regarded as almost sacred. Liberals could cite this tradition as they attempted to gain support in the Northern denominations from large middle parties not firmly committed. Thus began to break up the fundamentalist coalitions. Under strong pressure to disown the fundamentalists' avowed position of intolerance, many conservatives fell back. Only the most militant held to the logic that, if modernism was not eliminated, the churches must be

divided. This was the most effective countermove of the antifundamentalist forces in the Presbyterian Church.[18]

Perhaps this plea for toleration is best seen in Harry Emerson Fosdick's famous sermon, "Shall the Fundamentalists Win?" Fosdick, a famous liberal pastor in New York City, differentiated between two types of conservatives. He appealed to the tolerant group and castigated the intolerant fundamentalist group. Beginning with a look at Gamaliel's advice "to refrain from these men, lest we fight against God," Fosdick cautioned fundamentalists in their endeavor to cast liberalism out of their denomination.[19] He said:

> Already all of us must have heard about the people who call themselves the Fundamentalists. Their apparent intention is to drive out of the evangelical churches men and women of liberal opinions. . . . We should not identify the Fundamentalists with the conservatives. All Fundamentalists are conservativism, but not all conservatives are Fundamentalists. The best conservatives can often give lessons to the liberals in true liberality of spirit, but the Fundamentalist program is essentially illiberal [sic] and intolerant. The Fundamentalists see, and they see truly, that in this last generation there have been strange new movements in Christian thought.[20]

His appeal for toleration was in reality only a clearly laid out appeal for a continued inclusivism. Even more clever was the fashion in which he turned the table and plead with his own liberal fellow church men to tolerate those who held to the "fundamentals of the faith." He claimed:

> If a man is a genuine liberal, his primary protest is not against holding these opinions, although he may well protest against their being considered the fundamentals of Christianity. This is a free country and anybody has a right to hold these opinions or any others, if he is sincerely convinced of them. *The question is, Has anybody a right to deny the Christian name to those who differ with him on such points and to shut up against them the doors of Christian fellowship?* The Fundamentalists say that this must be done.

In this country and on the foreign field they are trying to do it.[21]

Indeed, the fundamentalists refused to hear the liberal's plea for tolerance because they considered the plea to come from professing but actually *unregenerate* "Christian" people. They held to the principle which Harold Lindsell would so eloquently articulate a few decades later: *"Peace at the expense of theological purity means a denial of what is foundational to the existence of the body."*[22]

Machen expresses very clearly the fundamentalists' point of contention: anyone who claims belief in key Christian doctrines and yet is still willing to unite with liberals who deny those doctrines is really one who regards those Christian doctrines as "trifles." He says:

> The case is similar with the liberal program for unity in the Church. It could never be advocated by anyone who had made the slightest effort to understand the point of view of his opponent in controversy. The liberal preacher says to the conservative party in the Church: "Let us unite in the same congregation, since of course doctrinal differences are trifles." But it is the very essence of "conservatism" in the Church to regard doctrinal differences as no trifles but as the matters of supreme moment. A man cannot possibly be an "evangelical" or a "conservative" (or, as he himself would say, simply a Christian) and regard the Cross of Christ as a trifle. To suppose that he can is the extreme of narrowness. It is not necessarily "narrow" to reject the vicarious sacrifice of our Lord as the sole means of salvation. It may be very wrong (and we believe that it is), but it is not necessarily narrow. But to suppose that a man can hold to the vicarious sacrifice of Christ and at the same time belittle that doctrine, to suppose that a man can believe that the eternal Son of God really bore the guilt of men's sins on the Cross and at the same time regard that belief as "trifle" without bearing upon the welfare of men's souls—that is very narrow and very absurd.[23]

TWISTING THE MEANING OF TOLERATION

The kind of tolerance the liberals were seeking was not a true type of tolerance. Genuine Baptists from the beginning were tolerant in that they never forced or coerced anyone to believe their doctrines. It is well known that *soul liberty* is a Baptist distinctive. Baptists have historically held that each individual is responsible before God and free to make his own choices and to practice religion according to his personal conviction. Baptists had a tremendous influence on the establishment of religious liberty in the United States. Throughout the centuries the Baptists often were those persecuted and at times killed by other religious groups (Catholics, puritans, congregationalists, etc.). It is these other groups who have in the past demonstrated genuine intolerance.

What the liberals actually wanted was not tolerance, but *acceptance.* They wanted fundamentalists to accept and recognize them as a legitimate part of Christianity. This is exactly what Fosdick pressed for in his question: "Has anybody a right to deny the Christian name to those who differ with him on such points and to shut up against them the doors of Christian fellowship?"

Fundamentalists who rejected the plea for "toleration" were not advocating *forcing* the liberals to change their opinions, but only disallowing the liberals to be recognized as legitimate within the body of saints. Thus anybody was free to deny Christ's deity, the atonement, and other fundamental doctrines, but he could not do so and rightfully remain in the body of those who believed those doctrines to be essential to Christianity.

However, as Marsden pointed out above, the plea for "toleration" found an ear in many conservatives. Likewise Price reports, "Perhaps more significant was the trend for some conservatives to accept an inclusive church as the means of obtaining peace and harmony."[24] In fact, key leaders among the early fundamentalist gatherings joined the liberals in this peace-proclaiming chorus. Curtis Lee Laws, editor of the conservative *Watchman-Examiner*, a broadly circulated Baptist magazine, reported with favor the fact that the 1923 convention was the first since 1919 to be conducted without controversy.[25] In 1926, the Northern Baptist Convention elected as president James Whitcomb Brougher, "a doctrinal conservative who favored forgetting the controversy with modernism. He toured the country advocating this position in a sermon titled, 'Play Ball.' "[26] Similarly, a "group of Presbyterian ministers sent forth a statement titled, 'A Plea for Peace and Work.' The plea stressed the need for unity among those who held diverse beliefs lest the progress of missions be hindered."[27]

EVANGELISTIC ZEAL VERSUS DOCTRINAL MILITANCY: A FALSE DICHOTOMY.

The majority of conservatives heard this plea for peace and work "lest the progress of missions be hindered." They did not want to see their missions endeavor slowed down because of doctrinal "squabbling."[28] These conservatives opted to keep the emphasis on "evangelism," even though this "evangelism" would be carried out at times by unbelieving liberal ministers.

In such a way, the pious approach of weighing evangelistic zeal against doctrinal militancy blinded many conservatives to the real issue. Blinded, they saw evangelistic zeal and doctrinal militancy as an *either/or* situation. But the real issue—the gospel itself—necessitates each believer to have *both* an evangelistic zeal *and* a doctrinal vigilance. For evangelistic zeal *without* doctrinal purity ceases to be *evangelistic* zeal. It merely becomes zeal for propagating a message, whether true or false.

Those who held in full to the biblical gospel not only considered their doctrinal militancy as defending this gospel, but showed zeal in propagating it. As Marsden admits, "Even among the most militant fundamentalists, soul-winning or missionary emphasis was mixed with their exclusivistic doctrinal vigilance."[29]

THE UNDERLYING FACTORS OF INCLUSIVISM

You might be tempted to ask: "How could some who embraced conservative theology accept the presence of liberals as full-fledged members of their Christian denomination?" The answer will unfold in the next few paragraphs.

1. *False Teaching: Not Heresy, Just Differing Views*

In pleading for "unity among those who held diverse beliefs,"[30] moderates began to *accept the deviant teachings* of the liberals merely as *views*, not as *heresy*. As Machen intimated earlier, when doctrines are rendered as "trifles," toleration to opposing views follows.

Significant in this regard is a discussion of the Auburn Affirmation:

> In reaction against the 1923 decisions that condemned Fosdick and reaffirmed the "five points," a group of ministers worked for several months following the General Assembly [of the Presbyterian Church] to draw up a public protest. In January 1924 they issued the "Auburn Affirmation" for which they secured some thirteen hundred signatures by the time of the 1924 Assembly.   This protest asserted, on constitutional grounds that had been upheld by progressive parties since 1729, that Presbyterian ministers had some liberty in interpreting the Westminister Confession of Faith, the church's official statement of Biblical teaching. Furthermore, the protest emphasized that the insistence on the inerrancy of Scripture, they said, went beyond both the Confession and the Bible's own statements. Furthermore, in its key passage, the Affirmation declared that the five-point declaration committed the church to "certain *theories*" concerning inspiration, the Incarnation, the Atonement, the Resurrection, and the supernatural power of Christ. Fellowship within the Presbyterian Chuuch [sic], the signers affirmed, should be *broad enough to include any people who like themselves held "most earnestly to these great facts and doctrines," regardless of the theories they employed to explain them.*
>
> Although most of the signers apparently held moderate or liberal theological positions, a few were known conservatives.[31]

What was the fruit of "this conservative-liberal coalition for 'peace and work,' culminating in the Auburn Affirmation"?[32] It "paved the way for the withdrawal in 1927 by the General Assembly of The Presbyterian Church, U.S.A., of its earlier stand for the five fundamentals."[33]

2. *Piety Serves As Criteria: Liberals Can Be Devout Christians*

Some moderates turned to an inclusive gospel when they began to consider the piety of certain liberals as evidence of genuine Christianity. This so-called piety is illustrated by Fosdick:

> We may well begin with the vexed and mooted question of the virgin birth of our Lord. I know people in the Christian churches, ministers, missionaries, laymen, devoted lovers of the Lord and servants of the Gospel, who, alike as they are in their personal devotion to the Master, hold quite different points of view about a matter like the virgin birth. . . . But, side by side with them in the evangelical churches is a group of equally loyal and reverent people who would say that the virgin birth is not to be accepted as an historic fact. . . . Is not the Christian Church large enough to hold within her hospitable fellowship people who differ on points like this and agree to differ until the fuller truth be manifested? The fundamentalists say not. They say the liberals must go. Well, if the Fundamentalists should succeed, then out of the Christian Church would go some of the best Christian life and consecration of his generation—multitudes of men and women, devout and reverent Christians, who need the Church and whom the Church needs.[34]

In light of this last quote, it is noteworthy to read what Goodchild states after critiquing Fosdick's book, The Modern Use of the Bible:

> It is very difficult for one who knows and loves Dr. Harry Fosdick to review a book by him. . . . His personality is so engaging, his spirit so buoyant, *his usual desire so evident to bring together the factions of distracted Christian people rather than to drive them apart, his passionate love for Jesus Christ is so conspicuous* that one is apt to think there can be nothing wrong with his teaching. . . . Yet The Modern Use of the Bible is a specious book. In it Dr. Fosdick declares his position as a modernist more clearly than is his habit. Yet he does it with such skill that he carries the average reader with him. His propositions appear reasonable and you find yourself assenting to them. But when you have finished with the book you realize that your Bible is gone, and your Savior is gone. You have Christ still as an ideal, as a teacher and an

> example, but that is all—and that is a very poor "all" indeed
> for men who bear a burden of guilt that must be put away.[35]

Goodchild paints Fosdick as one who loves Christ and seeks to labor for the unity between Christians. Writing from the point of view of a moderate conservative, Professor Norman Maring has not missed the significance of Goodchild's opinion of Fosdick. To Maring this illustrated a different spirit than would have portrayed a militant fundamentalist: "one can hardly picture the fundamentalist as he is ordinarily caricatured today admitting that Dr. Fosdick had a 'passionate love for Jesus Christ'!"[36] However, how could Goodchild say that of one whom he knows does not believe in the same Christ? Has Fosdick's apparent piety seduced Goodchild?

Obviously Maring himself has also followed Goodchild in embracing an inclusive viewpoint. First note his awareness of the issues and the stand he claims to hold regarding the gospel:

> The case of the Fundamentalists [the moderate ones] was a reasonable one. They stood essentially where Baptists had stood a generation before, and it was the new generation which was asking for new definitions and interpretations. Nor did these Fundamentalists oppose progress and change; they were willing to tolerate many points of disagreement. They did not object to Biblical criticism so long as it was carried on in a reverent spirit, and they were willing to permit considerable latitude in interpretations of theological doctrines. However, it was their contention that theology was moving in the direction of a naturalism which undermined the very gospel itself. . . . The moderate conservatives represented by Dr. Laws and Dr. Goodchild were willing that Baptists should have freedom to interpret the Scriptures for themselves. However, when theological interpretation involved a denial of the essential message of the Bible, it was time to protest. . . . To focus attention upon single points like the Virgin Birth, the authority of the Bible, the resurrection, the atonement, or the second coming is to be unable to see the forest because of the trees. *The question of salvation is what is really at stake.*[37]

But secondly, and more importantly, note how he qualifies his stand for the gospel. He says: "To say that liberalism constituted a threat to the gospel does not mean that we must discredit the men who honestly faced difficult issues courageously. *Many liberals were devout Christians.*"[38]

Perhaps he says it best when he states:

> On the whole, [the moderate fundamentalists] had a sense of the vital core of the gospel and maintained it in the face of a Modernism which in its desire to keep abreast of the times *almost* dissolved its message.   Of course, not all Fundamentalists were as open-minded or as well informed as these men, but they were the accepted leaders and spokesmen, and represent the main thrust of organized Fundamentalism in the Northern Baptist Convention during the early 1920s.[39]

This word "almost" made the whole difference between a militant fundamentalist and a conservative moderate.   To the true fundamentalist, liberalism had not just "almost" lost the message, it had definitely and *completely* lost it. Therefore, any piety they showed was only apparent and not an indication of a relationship with the Savior Jesus Christ!

3. *Simplification and Redefinition of the Gospel*

Underlying the inclusive modus operandi was a *simplification* and *redefinition* of the gospel itself.   The Hartley case will serve as an illustration.

When M. R. Hartley, a missionary to Asia, was home on furlough in 1924, he reported to the Foreign Board of the NBC that he no longer believed in the deity of Christ. "The board voted nine to four to keep him on as a 'sound man,' which hardly seemed to [militant] conservatives like examining candidates 'very carefully as to their belief regarding Christ and the Bible,' as the convention president had claimed the boards were doing."[40]   The fundamentalists questioned "this practice of inclusivism, [but] the Foreign Board's chairman, professor Frederick L. Anderson of Newton Theological Institution, *ardently defended the inclusive policy as being 'within the limits of the Gospel.'* "[41]   Anderson was a conservative who had even "addressed the historic gathering in Buffalo that organized the Fundamentalist Fellowship in 1920."[42]   Though Anderson himself believed in the Lord's deity, he fought for an inclusive gospel which would permit Christ's deity to be denied.

Therefore, no longer were some key doctrines (i.e. the deity and atonement of Christ) absolutely crucial to the gospel. This liberal-evangelical inclusivism was supposedly "within the limits of the Gospel."

Curtis Lee Laws is also very explicit on this issue. In an editorial entitled "Are Modernists Christians?" he argues against Dr. A. Slaten who had asserted in one of his sermons that "modernism is not Christianity." Slaten's argument was "that since Christianity means the reception as truth of a 'certain accepted scheme of thought', and since the modernist declines to receive this, the modernist is not a Christian."[43] Laws did not agree at all with the definition on which Dr. Slaten rested his argument. He states in his editorial:

> To be a Christian means much more than an intellectual assent to a prescribed scheme of things. The Christian is a man who through faith in Jesus Christ has received into his heart and life the Saviour's love, and who is directed in all matters of conduct, in the shaping of his character, and in his intercourse with God and men, by the power of the Holy Ghost. If he have [sic] not come into fellowship with Jesus Christ through faith in him as the only begotten Son of God, he is certainly not a Christian; and he should have the courage to dissociate himself from any church to which this faith and fellowship are the vital terms of membership.[44]

While the modernist claimed belief in Christ as the Son of God, he did so with a totally different understanding than the fundamentalist. He did not acknowledge Christ as eternal Deity! The crucial point is that, to the inclusivists, a claim of belief no longer had to be verified with a proper biblical definition of terms. To them, those definitions were only matters of opinion and personal interpretation.

This is precisely why Laws, in other articles, could profess to still be "fighting" for conservatism while at the same time be rejoicing in liberal/conservative denominational unity.[45] This also explains clearly how many could talk peace while still pushing for a conservative agenda. Thus, the evangelical inclusivists pressed for their conservative views on the gospel, while not making them necessary for Christian fellowship.

THE EFFECTS OF INCLUSIVISM: LIBERAL ADVANCEMENT

This adoption of inclusivism made the moderate conservatives allies with the liberals in their fight against fundamentalism. This was evident to the modernists, as Price relates:

> Fundamentalists differed from conservatives on the question of inclusivism. An editorial in the *Christian Century* [a liberal magazine] made the sharpest distinction between fundamentalists and modernists, but with the conservatives the liberal *Christian Century* saw only "the range of intellectual differences within a common fellowship." Thus liberals wooed conservatives as allies in the campaign for an inclusive church.[46]

In fact, it may better be said, as Marsden outlines in his book, that the *underlying* battle in the liberal-fundamental controversy was not between liberalism and fundamentalism, but rather between *inclusivism* and *exclusivism*.[47]   Sadly, inclusivism won and the mainline denominational ships continued to sink in the sea of heresy.[48]

Kirsopp Lake perhaps gave much insight when he said:

> The Experimentalist [the liberal] could go ahead much faster if he took the advice showered on him by the Fundamentalists and cut himself loose from all affiliation with the existing churches. . . . But if he has—as I have—any real affection for the institutions of his fathers, he will steadily postpone following this advice so long as he can. He will do best to stay where he is, in whatever church it may be, and by his frank and sometimes painful criticism, help the Institutionalists [the moderate conservatives], who as a rule are far more capable of seeing what is expedient or necessary for the moment and are less troubled by questions of verbal accuracy. He will not receive an official vote of thanks for his pains; but in private *the Institutionalist will admit that he could never have resisted Fundamentalist pressure, had not the flagrant and outspoken heresy of the Experimentalist made his own position appear conservative by contrast.*[49]

It is therefore, not surprising, nor troubling, to know that the militant fundamentalists held more respect for the liberals than for the conservatives who fought for an inclusive church. "Fosdick, says fundamentalist T. T. Shields, at least wore the uniform of the enemy."[50]

THE SUBTLETY OF INCLUSIVISM

Unfortunately, inclusivism is a breed of heresy which comes in very deceptive form. It is like a large nebulous creature, whose tentacles spread far and wide among many, even among some who profess their antagonism toward it. The matter relating to the Inclusive Policy of the NBC serves well the purpose of illustrating the subtlety of inclusivism. Adopted officially on October 19, 1923, the Inclusive Policy read as follows:

> Our denomination, our Society, and our churches have always given to officers, missionaries, and pastors a considerable degree of liberty of theological opinion. . . . It has not been our Baptist custom to limit too explicitly the form in which these doctrines must be held and expressed.
> . . . The Board, composed like our churches of men and women of diverse opinions, has heretofore included and should include among its officers and missionaries representatives of various elements among our people.[51]

The Inclusive Policy guaranteed that no segment of the Baptist denomination could ensure what doctrinal stance the Convention missionaries and workers had to take. Many conservatives who remained in the denomination after the fundamentalist defeats of the 20s still had great trouble with the Inclusive Policy and opposed sending out liberal missionaries. Conservatives made many efforts to stop the inclusive practice of the American Baptist Foreign Mission Society (ABFMS), the foreign mission agency of the NBC.

While apparently opposing inclusivism, this attempt itself involved accepting a degree of inclusivism. Chester Tulga was most articulate in exposing the error and inherent inclusivism of such efforts. With pointed accuracy, Tulga argues that since the Convention was inclusive as a whole, not only in practice but officially, it would not be right for the conservatives to allow only conservative representatives of the Convention on the mission field. Such a move would be non-democratic:

> To ask the ABFMS to send out missionaries holding to one theological viewpoint only, is to ask it to abandon representative character and to refuse a large portion of its contributing constituency any representation in its policies or its personnel.[52]

Even worse, such a move would not acknowledge the root problem of being in a denomination with full-fledged liberal members.[53] This conservative coalition accepted inclusivism on the home front while claiming it was a problem on the foreign field. The president of the Convention himself showed more wisdom than many NBC conservatives of that time. As the *Baptist Bulletin* reports:

> On the platform of the Convention in Milwaukee, we personally heard the President of the Board defend this policy [the inclusive policy of the ABFMS Board]. His argument was that since Modernism and Fundamentalism, alike, are accepted in the Northern Baptist Convention, and they and their churches are in good standing, the Board, as an agency of the Convention, has no right to discriminate between them. He said, in effect, if distinctions are to be made and barriers made, *the place to set them up is at the front door* of the Convention, not at the door to the mission field.[54]

How true and consistent, but unfortunately, the majority of fundamentalists who had come to that conclusion had already left the denomination following the inclusivists' victories of the 1920s.

Unfortunately, the solution to which many turned was the creation of the Conservative Baptist Foreign Mission Society (CBFMS). Seemingly promising, this society was to ensure the sending out of only conservative missionaries. However, the conservative coalition created the CBFMS to function *within* the NBC for the purpose of opposing the Inclusive Policy of the ABFMS.[55] Thus, inclusivism on the home front was still not rejected. Therefore, inclusivism was not only a major problem in the fundamentalist defeats of the 1920s, but it was also deeply embedded in many who expressed opposition to the Inclusive Policy of the ABFMS.

CONCLUSION

The outcome of the liberal-fundamentalist controversy during the early part of this century was not determined by either of those camps. Rather, it was decided by an inclusive middle party. By their inclusivism, these conservative moderates gave liberals a legitimate place within the fellowship of the Protestant denominations. Their inclusivism inherently meant understanding the deviant teachings of the liberals only as views, opinions and matters of personal interpretation—no matter how false they were thought to be. Thus, a subtle redefinition of the gospel and of essential Christianity determined the outcome of the controversy. Ultimately, those who were inclusive accepted a generic claim to believing in Christ and an appearance of piety as sufficient grounds to be considered part of the family of God. Therefore, you can see how in the early years of this century, evangelical inclusivism undermined the *gospel* it claimed to uphold by turning into *mere **opinions*** the very *elements* of the biblical gospel.

Militant fundamentalists had a real cause. Upholding the biblical gospel meant not only rejecting the liberalism of false teachers, but also rejecting the evangelical inclusivism of avowed conservatives. In fact, this evangelical inclusivism was more dangerous and *destructive* than the outright liberalism of that time, for it is inclusivism that *bridged the gap* between sound doctrine and false teaching.

This era in the history of the Church reminds us of the vital issues that are affected by evangelical inclusivism. It is the subtle poison of inclusivism more than the direct frontal attacks of heresy that have silenced the major protestant denominations in their evangelical witness.

Logically, the inclusive-evangelical policy is a contradiction, for the inclusive policy cancels out the evangelical policy. The two parts of this statement, analyzed objectively, are mutually contradictory.   — Chester Tulga[56]

NOTES ON CHAPTER 1

1. Oliver Price, "Historical Background of the Five Fundamentals," *Bibliotheca Sacra* (January 1961): 39.

2. The liberal preacher Fosdick also suggests this himself in his sermon, "Shall the Fundamentalists Win?" when he says, "I speak of them [the fundamentalists] the more freely because there are no two denominations more affected by them than the Baptist and the Presbyterian" [Sermon reprint in *Christian Work* CXII (June 10, 1922): 716-22]. See also George M. Marsden, Fundamentalism and American Culture (Oxford: Oxford University Press, 1980), 180.

3. Cf. Ernest R. Sandeen, The Roots of Fundamentalism (Grand Rapids: Baker Book House, 1978; reprint from University of Chicago, 1970), 263.

4. See Marsden, Fundamentalism and American Culture, 164; Norman Maring, "Conservative But Progressive," in What God Hath Wrougth, ed. Gilbert L. Guffin (Chicago: Judson Press, 1960), 22.

5. Kirsopp Lake, The Religion of Yesterday and Tomorrow (Boston: Houghton Mifflin, 1925), 61-62.

6. Supernaturalism is the belief that God can manifest Himself through special revelation or supernatural miracles in the course of life on earth.

7. J. Gresham Machen, Christianity and Liberalism (Grand Rapids: Wm. B. Eerdmans Publishing Co, 1946), 2.

8. Ibid.

9. Ibid., 7.

10. Lake, Religion of Yesterday and Tomorrow, 64-67. Lake states:
    The Experimentalist, then, holds that there are two great experiments in life which are the basis of religion. . . . [The first] is made when a man is conscious that there is a purpose in life of which he is only a part, but with which he can cooperate if he choose, *and he does choose*. . . . The Experimentalist deserves his name not because he holds the view that there is a purpose in life--that is theory--but because, believing that there is this purpose, he chooses to make the experiment of becoming its servant. Is there any difference in quality between the Experimentalist who does this and the primitive Christian who consecrated himself to the Kingdom of God? The attitude of mind is the same as that which said, "Thy will, not mine, be done." The difference is that the Experimentalist, especially if he is outside the churches, wishes to state his own experiment, and the theory which underlies it, in his own language. After he has done so, he is able to recognize the value and the beauty of the language of the past, even though he cannot make that language his own, for the **theory** of the past is not the same as his own. **If the Fundamentalist is allowed**

to maintain his position that the membership in the Church means the acceptance of a definite theory, the Experimentalist will stay outside or go outside the Church. . . .

[The second] is made when a man is conscious that there is a source of life which imparts help to him when he is weak, comfort when he is in sorrow, and purification when he has sinned. . . . Religion requires men who will make the experiments, and record them faithfully and intelligibly, not those who repeat other people's formulae [sic], and force their results to agree with them. Experimentalists claim the right to continue in the churches, and feel that the claim of the Fundamentalist to exclude them is based on a radically wrong conception which has survived from an earlier age. The Churches are not societies for the preservation of **ancient opinions**, but for the furtherance of living religion [italics original; bold emphasis added] .

11. Ibid.

12. Ibid., emphasis added.

13. Ibid.

14. This was before the term "fundamentalist" included strains of separatism. At that time, fundamentalists were basically concerned conservatives. Two groups emerged from this group: the separatist fundamentalists, and the conservative moderates who stayed within the denomination.

15. Lake, Religion of Yesterday and Tomorrow, 68-69.

16. Frank M. Goodchild, "Dr. Fosdick's 'Modern Use of the Bible,' " *Watchman Examiner* (February 19, 1925): 235; see also Maring, "Conservative but Progressive," 26-27.

17. David O. Beale, In Pursuit of Purity (Greenville, SC: Unusual Publications, 1986), 174.

18. Marsden, Fundamentalism and American Culture, 180.

19. If some are unfamiliar with Fosdick, his own sermon reflects well his liberalism:

[The Fundamentalists] insist that we must all believe in the historicity of certain special miracles, pre-eminently the virgin birth our Lord; that we must believe in a special theory of inspiration--that the original documents of the Scripture, which of course we no longer possess, were inerrantly dictated to men a good deal as a man might dictate to a stenographer; that we must believe in a special theory of the atonement--that the blood of our Lord, shed in a substitutionary death, placates an alienated Deity and makes possible welcome for the returning sinner; and that we must believe in the second coming of our Lord upon the clouds of heaven to set up a millennium here, as the only way in which God can bring history to a worthy denouement. Such are some of the stakes which are being driven to mark a deadline of doctrine around the Church [Harry Emerson Fosdick, "Shall the Fundamentalists Win?" Sermon reprint in *Christian Work* CXII (June 10, 1922): 716-22; 717].

20. Ibid., 716.

21. Ibid., 717, emphasis added.

22. Harold Lindsell, The Bible in the Balance (Grand Rapids: Zondervan Publishing House, 1979), 17.

23. Machen, Christianity and Liberalism, 161-62.

24. Price, "Historical Background of the Five Fundamentals," 38-39.

25. Laws, illustrating well Lake's definition of Institutionalist, reports:

This was the first convention since the Denver meeting in which there was no conflict between the conservative and liberal wings of the denomination. . . . The newly elected officers are eminently satisfactory. The organization, which will next year succeed the General Board of Promotion, meets the approval of everybody. It preserves the principle of co-operation, but safeguards the autonomy of the societies. . . . The denomination, sadly divided by the Denver Convention, has been brought together again by the wisdom of this Convention. . . . It will have to be conceded that many ardent fundamentalists were disappointed that "nothing was done" at Atlantic City [the location of the 1923 Convention]. Some insisted that a confession of faith should be presented. Some resented the appearance of ultra-liberals on the program and applauded even the protest of Dr. Straton against the appearance of President Faunce. But the majority of the fundamentalists were satisfied with the Convention and rejoiced in the unmistakable evidence of their influence in the plans and programs of the Convention. The program for future work embraces practically everything that conservatism has contended for. The Convention and the denomination will know that the fight against heresy in our pulpits and against rationalism in our schools at home and abroad will go right on. . . . Those who have put their hands to the plow will never turn back. On the other hand, there is general rejoicing that we have adopted a program for future work in which all can unite, for we are all Baptists, and all of us alike love our denomination. . . . An amazing amount of hard work is done by the boards and committees of the Convention. . . . We may well rejoice that we have so many capable and consecrated men and women who are willing to give their time, their thought and their energy to our work. . . . The secretaries or our Societies and Boards do not have an enviable task. . . . Our secretaries are not perfect, but they are good and true men, doing a noble and self-sacrificing work. Let us thank God for them and give them our heartiest co-operation [Curtis L. Laws, "Convention Sidelights" *Watchman Examiner* (June 7, 1923): 706].

26. Price, "Historical Background of the Five Fundamentals," 38-39.

27. Ibid., 38-39.

28. See Beale, In Pursuit of Purity, 215-216, and Marsden, Fundamentalism and American Culture, 181-83. For instance, Beale says of Anderson, "Such moderate conservatives within the NBC, while considering themselves Fundamentalists, were demonstrating that when said and done their doctrinal militancy was simply not as strong as their zeal for spreading the gospel [216]." Similarly, Marsden says: "As the [NBC] convention speaker, Massee affirmed the ideals of the revivalist tradition with sentiments reminiscent of Dwight L. Moody, calling for a moratorium on debate in order to get to the main business of soul-winning. Perhaps it was the tension between these two conflicting emphases--the fight against apostasy on the one hand, soul-winning on the other--that kept many potential fundamentalists from full identification with fundamentalist attitudes [181]." He also later says: "Both [inclusivists and

exclusivists] were militant to a degree, although some of the original fundamentalists defected once the consequences for evangelism became apparent [183]." The problem with Beale's and Marsden's statements is that they apparently concur with the dichotomy between evangelistic zeal and doctrinal vigilance that the moderates saw. Such should not be! Without doctrinal purity, the zeal for the gospel becomes the zeal for a corrupt or false gospel; and there cannot be any zeal for the biblical gospel without making sure that it is the biblical gospel that is being preached.

29. Marsden, 181.

30. Price, "Historical Background of the Five Fundamentals," 38-39.

31. See "AN AFFIRMATION: Designed to safeguard the unity and liberty of the Presbyterian Church in the United States of America," reprinted in *The Presbyterian* XCIV (January 17, 1924): 6-7, emphasis added. Cf. Charles E. Quirk, "Origins of the Auburn Affirmation," *Journal of Presbyterian History* LIII (Summer, 1975): 120-142.

32. Price, "Historical Background of the Five Fundamentals," 39-40.

33. Ibid.

34. Fosdick, "Shall the Fundamentalists Win?" 717-718.

35. Goodchild, "Dr. Fosdick's 'Modern Use of the Bible,' " 235, emphasis added.

36. Maring, "Conservative But Progressive," 38.

37. Ibid., 26-27, emphasis added.

38. Ibid., 37, emphasis added.

39. Ibid., 39, emphasis added.

40. Beale, In Pursuit of Purity, 215; cf. *Watchman-Examiner* (June 12, 1924): 749.

41. Ibid., emphasis added.

42. Ibid.

43. Curtis Lee Laws, "Are Modernists Christians?" Editorial note in the *Watchman Examiner* (January 7, 1926): 7.

44. Ibid.

45. Laws says for instance, "The Convention and the denomination will know that the fight against heresy in our pulpits and against rationalism in our schools at home and abroad will go right on. . . . *On the other hand, there is general rejoicing that we have adopted a program for future work in which all can unite, for we are all Baptists, and all of us alike love our denomination*" [Laws, "Convention Sidelights," 706, emphasis added].

46. Price, "Historical Background of the Five Fundamentals," 39.

47. Marsden, Fundamentalism and American Culture, 181-184.

48. For this very reason, some militant fundamentalists had more respect for the liberals than for the inclusive conservatives [Marsden, 182].

49. Lake, The Religion of Yesterday and Tomorrow, 72, emphasis added.

50. As quoted by Marsden, Fundamentalism and American Culture, 182.

51. As quoted in Beale, 215 from the *Watchman-Examiner* (November 15, 1923): 1468.

52. Chester Earl Tulga, The Story of the Inclusive Policy of American Baptist Foreign Mission Society, 1923-1944; a Study of Theological Deception (Chicago: Conservative Baptist Fellowship of Northern Baptists, [194?]), 122ff.

53. Ibid.

54. Van Gilder, H. O., ed., "The Irrefutable Logic of the Inclusive Policy," *Baptist Bulletin* (May 1946): 1, emphasis added.

55. The NBC never did let the CBFMS function as part of the NBC.

56. Tulga, The Story of the Inclusive Policy of American Baptist Foreign Mission Society, 120.

Chapter 2

THE CHANGING OF THE TIDE
-- THE CASE OF BILLY GRAHAM

The gospel that built this school and the gospel that brings me here tonight is still the way of salvation. . . .
—Billy Graham to his Roman Catholic
audience at Belmont Abbey.[1]

W HEN ORTHODOXY in the mainline denominations died out, one could have expected the decline of the *evangelical* type of inclusivism. Losing their evangelical voice, the mainline denominations would be left with a flourishing inclusivism for sure, but less and less of an *evangelical* kind. However, when the mainline denominations renounced their orthodoxy and evangelical voice, this special *evangelical* type of inclusivism did not die away. The germ spread into the camp of those that had come out of the mainline denominations. It spread into the fundamental-evangelical arena with the birth of the New-evangelical movement—now simply known as the evangelical movement. Particularly significant in this regard is the influence of one of the main leaders of New-evangelicalism, Billy Graham.

The case of Billy Graham is not one to have gone unnoticed in this century. He is known as an evangelist not only throughout North America, but also throughout the world. Evangelicals herald him as one of their greatest evangelists, while fundamentalists have long believed him to be a "compromiser." Many fundamentalists do, however, rejoice at his gospel, though they balk at his ecumenical methods.

Unfortunately, I fear, many have not listened closely to his message. Over the last fifty years, Billy Graham has increasingly demonstrated what he stands for, what he believes in and what he is pushing for. The problem is not simply that of compromise, as has long been held by fundamentalists. It goes much deeper and involves the very nature of the gospel Graham preaches.

At this point, the evangelical reader might be tempted to simply dismiss this book, thinking, "How can any genuine Christian not stand behind Billy Graham's simple and clear message of salvation?" But this reaction is expected and in fact reinforces my thesis concerning *evangelical* inclusivism. Graham's claim to be evangelical is evident to all. But equally evident is an inclusivism that ultimately redefines the *evangel* (gospel) he preaches.

GRAHAM'S MESSAGE AND BELIEFS

It is common knowledge that Graham came out of fundamentalist circles in the 1950s. Even militant fundamentalist William B. Riley had seen hope in the young Graham when he called him to be his successor as president of the then-fundamentalist Northwestern schools [1948-1952]. But quickly Graham's real direction and beliefs surfaced, already becoming evident as early as 1957 during the famous New York Crusade. In his sympathetic biography, author Ralph Martin reports at length on the direction Graham chose to go from the 1950s on:

> The fundamentalists' rage increased as plans for the
> New York crusade moved forward. As the committees took

shape, it became clear that Graham did indeed plan to hold an ecumenical crusade. One critic charged that of the 140 people on the General Crusade Committee, at least 120 were "reputed to be modernists, liberals, infidels, or something other than fundamental". . . .

Graham further manifested his ostensible lack of concern for sound doctrine not only by such statements as "the one badge of Christian discipleship is not orthodoxy, but love," but also by his apparent willingness to send decision cards to Catholic and Jewish clergy. . . . If an inquirer specifically asked to be referred to a Catholic church or Jewish synagogue, that request would be honored. "After all," he explained, "I have no quarrel with the Catholic Church. Christians are not limited to any church. The only question is: are you committed to Christ?"

As a further sign he was veering to the left, Graham began to accept invitations to speak at liberal seminaries. At Colgate Rochester Divinity School, he attempted to bridge the differences between his own theology and that of the eminent neoorthodox theologian and social ethnic, Reinhold Niebuhr. When he spoke of "the central need for a personal experience of Jesus Christ," he added, as if they were synonymous conceptions, "or what Niebuhr would call an encounter with the living God." A Fundamentalist reporting on this event objected that "no one in his right mind would believe for a moment that what the neo-orthodox Niebuhr means by 'an encounter with the living God' and what Jesus Christ defined as being 'born again' are one and the same."[2]

At New York's Union Theological Seminary, Graham had the temerity to say kind words about "known liberals," including his old friend Chuck Templeton, who was then serving as an evangelist for the National Council of Churches. His hobnobbing with Anglicans in Great Britain and with Church of Scotland pastors in Glasgow added fuel to the fire. To make matters worse, he had invited some prominent American liberals, including New York pastor John Sutherland Bonnell, who publicly acknowledged that he did not believe in the Trinity, the Virgin Birth, the Resurrection, the inerrancy of Scripture, or heaven and hell, to sit on the platform with him during some of the services at Kelvin Hall. When Scottish reporters tried to pin down Graham's location on the contemporary spectrum, he declared, in a statement that mightily offended his

> conservative critics, "I am neither a fundamentalist nor a
> modernist." To make matters worse, he told another
> reporter, "The ecumenical movement has broadened my
> viewpoint and I recognize now that God has his people in all
> churches."[3]

Graham's broadening view should not be news. It has been evident for the last forty years. But, what I would like to point out is the significance of Graham's views. His views are not just a demonstration of a lack of understanding on the principles of biblical separation, as most fundamentalists maintain. The issue is far greater than any lack of separation on Graham's part. Graham's broad views, over the years, have increasingly revealed the outlines of a gospel defined by its inclusivism.

> Graham's ever-widening acceptance of others who professed
> to be Christians manifested itself not only in his continued
> association with the World Council of Churches—he
> attended its general assembly in New Delhi in 1961 at the
> council's invitation—but also in an improved relationship
> with Catholics, especially after John XXIII assumed the
> papal chair.[4]

GRAHAM'S APPROACH TO CATHOLICS:
THEY ARE PART OF THE FOLD

Some have understood that Graham has worked with Catholics and other non-evangelicals in order to win them.[5] So how does he see the Catholics, and liberals with whom he works at times? Does he see them as people he needs to reach at any cost, even at the cost of having them sit on his platform? When I attended one of his crusades as a simple observer, Graham mentioned praying with a Catholic archbishop. Was it to reach the Catholic archbishop that Graham mentioned how sweet a time of prayer he enjoyed having with him? Some may want to believe that, but such a belief cannot be based on anything Graham has indicated concerning his relationship with the Catholic clergy with whom he has worked.

Despite acknowledged differences between Catholicism and his evangelical theology, Graham sees orthodox Catholics as being within the family of God. A perusal of Pollock's authorized biography of Graham's decisive years makes this evident. Also, with an approving voice, *Christianity Today* reported on Graham's address to Roman Catholic Belmont Abbey College: "One thing good has come out of it though, he told his audience of nearly 1,500: 'We can talk to one another as Christian brothers.' "[6]

And what about Graham's thoughts on the pope? This is an interesting question, since it does not deal with American Catholicism, but with the very leader of the Roman Catholic religious system.[7] Reflecting on some differences between Catholicism and his own theology, he says:

> The infallibility of the pope is something Protestants can never accept, but I have a great deal of admiration for the pope, even though I don't accept all of his theology. *I don't think the differences are important as far as personal salvation is concerned.*[8]

Has the pope suddenly become evangelical? Has he repudiated the sacramental view of salvation taught for centuries by the Roman Catholic Church? Not for a second.[9] Perhaps the clearest statement from Graham is one he recently reasserted: "I have found that my beliefs are essentially the same as those of orthodox Roman Catholics."[10]

GRAHAM'S VIEW OF CONVERSION

How does one explain this obvious inclusivism? The answer will become clear when you understand Graham's view of conversion. His view, as given at length below, permits a compatibility between the evangelical type of conversion and the Roman Catholic type of conversion (which they call Christian nurture).

> The idea of conversion is often a difficult problem to those who hold a high view of sacramental grace. Many of the theologians and clergy cannot accept the idea of personal conversion on the part of those who were baptized in infancy. However, I have been agreeably surprised at the number of theologians and clergy who have successfully bridged this

gap and successfully overcome this problem.   Many Anglicans, Lutherans, Presbyterians, Orthodox and even Roman Catholic clergy have agreed that those within the Church need "converting" even after baptism and confirmation. The question I want to raise is this: is the theology of adult conversion fundamentally different from that of a child who is cradled in the faith and nurtured in the arms of the Church? *It is my opinion that we ought not to contrast the "nurture of grace" and the "grace of conversion" as many have tried to do.* I am convinced that there are both, and happy is the man who by the nurture of grace is brought to the grace of conversion. *Conversion can be an ultimate and proper fulfillment of all that baptism meant to the child, and perhaps later even in confirmation. Conversion must express itself in life as a change of mind, a radical break in the past, and a total commitment to Christ for the future. Whether conversion happens suddenly in adulthood or gradually through childhood is beside the point. The thing that counts is that it happens. . . .*

This is the greatest problem facing the Church today! The deep motivating spiritual power is almost non-existent! *If confirmation as it is usually understood is followed to its logical conclusion it can and often does become conversion.* However, I am convinced that in tens of thousands of cases baptism and confirmation have become only a "form." They have led many to believe that they need no further experience and no further relationship with God. . . . There are millions of professing Christians who have had just enough religion to inoculate themselves against a genuine relationship with Christ. The point I am trying to make is that in thousands of cases Biblical conversion is needed even after Baptism and confirmation, *to give meaning and reality to the earlier experience.*[11]

Significantly, Graham says that baptism and confirmation are legitimate ways through which one can enter into relationship with God. True, he says that often conversion needs to follow, but then, as you will notice, if a biblical conversion is needed, it is only "to give meaning and reality to the earlier experience."

This view is not a recent modification in his view, several years ago Graham said in a 1961 interview with the Lutheran Standard:

> I do believe that something happens at the baptism of an infant . . . we cannot fully understand the mysteries of God, but I believe that a miracle can happen in these children so that they are regenerated, that is, made Christian, through infant baptism.[12]

Graham's teaching on baptism and confirmation should alarm any true evangelical.

Graham does not stress this in his crusade messages, but evidences of his inclusivism on conversion are there—and Catholics are not deaf to such a position. Even as early as 1970, one Catholic writer, Carolo W. Dullea, saw that Graham's message was inclusive enough to make room for their theology. Dullea has pointed out:

> Nowhere does Graham suppose that conversion is a once-for-all event. Not only can this new life be lost, but it is capable of indefinite degrees of development. He quotes II Cor (4:7) "We have this treasure in earthen vessels," and notes that we are not delivered completely yet, that our final completion will be in heaven. Once converted we have to keep striving, even in spite of our falls, toward what John Wesley called "sanctification" or "perfect love."[13]

Catholics admittedly emphasize the nurturing aspect of faith much more than does Graham. Catholic author J. Baille gives account of the Catholic view of conversion:

> The Catholic however is very conscious, undoubtedly more than an evangelical of Graham's style, of the fact that this basic decision does not remain once-for-all and irrevocably "decided," that it needs constant renewal, rectification, and even re-ratification after violation. The Catholic has no illusions about perfectionism in "the saints." He is painfully conscious that even the most fervent, subjectively unconditional "decisions for Christ" can and unfortunately often are nullified subsequently by the inconsistent, miserably peccable human beings who make them. He has no "assurance of salvation" in any Wesleyan sense, even though

he has complete reliance on God's promises. He would temper Graham's optimism about the moral capabilities of the born-again Christian. He would qualify and tend to minimize the reliance on the single act of decision, the stress on the one-time crisis conversion as a guarantee or even a promise of a life that will be lived for ever after "in Christ." He would endorse John Baillie's sage critique of "one single conversional readjustment" and his quoting with approval of the saying, "the Christian life is made up of ever new beginnings."[14]

Dullea clearly sums up what Graham communicates to them in his messages:

> In justice to Graham, he himself does not make Christian conversion consist in this one only act, "decision for Christ." He says, as noted above, that it is not a once-for-all experience, but a step. However, he does not say this very often, nor very loudly. It is question of emphasis. In truth, he seems to want it both ways, both a once-and-for-all crisis-type decision that he presumes will remain fixed (aided of course by prayer and Bible reading), as well as a process-type conversion that is typified by nurture and gradual growth. *Graham admits both kinds of conversion. On this point he is not a doctrinaire evangelical.*[15]

Graham's recent message on loneliness during the Twin Cities Crusade of 1996 illustrates well what Dullea says of Graham. Here are some key sections of that message:

> There is another person in the universe called the devil, and the devil does not want you to know God, because he knows that if you know Christ as your Lord and Savior He'll meet that longing and empty void in your heart that brings about loneliness. You go to church, some of you, you've been baptized, you've been confirmed, and all of that is good. What you ought to do is reconfirm your confirmation vows. Reconfirm what happened in baptism, and say, "Oh Lord I want to come back, I want to come back, wholly, back in the fellowship" and He'll open his arms and receive you. . . . How many of us have gone away from God after being faithful to Him for awhile, and there was a time that you

knew the fellowship of God's people. You had peace with God. You've found him through baptism and confirmation, but you've went [sic] out from the presence of God . . . you long to have that same joy that you had years ago. And you would like to come back. Tonight is the night to come back.
. . .

There is only one remedy for loneliness that you feel in your life and your heart. Through Jesus Christ, we can have the most fundamental relationship in life *restored*. Tonight, you don't have to wait till you go to church next Sunday . . . say, "Yes, Lord Jesus, come in. . . ."

I am going to ask you to get up out of your seats, right now, hundreds of you and say tonight: "I want to experience Christ; I want him in my heart; I want him in my life, I want him to be my Savior, my Lord, and my Master. I want to renew my fellowship with him." If you've never come to Christ, never made a commitment, this is for you *too*. If you have another religious background, it's for you, it's for everybody. Hundreds of you, God is speaking to you. . . ."[16]

In that message, therefore, he clearly acknowledges the sacramental type of Christian nurture with its inherent need for continuance—lest there be falling away of God's presence. For those that have fallen away, they need to come back to Christ, and those that have never made a commitment to Christ need to do so for the first time.

In his sermon, Graham at times seems to suggest a loss of salvation for those that have fallen away after their baptism or confirmation. But even if rededication means coming back into fellowship rather than to a saving relationship with Christ, *truth is not proclaimed*. For either possibility is based on the assumption that baptism and/or confirmation has brought one into fellowship with God. This cancels out the biblical truth that one is totally lost before he turns to God in personal faith and in faith alone (Eph. 2:1-10).

REDEDICATIONS

Invariably then, Graham's organization often considers those that come with church backgrounds as simply coming for rededication. There is no need to repudiate one's past religious experiences and beliefs. A Catholic does not need to repudiate his baptism or any of his Catholic sacramental theology. A liberal does not need to think that he had no part of Christ before. One can just come for a renewed experience of personal fellowship with Christ. Take for example, the following accounts:

> In the Communist-dominated city of Katowice, where nearly 6,500—a high percentage of them young people—jammed into the cathedral, a corps of approximately 300 priests and nuns sitting together in a high balcony watched skeptically. As Graham rose to speak, a priest said to a colleague, "Now the show is to begin." When the evangelist finished his sermon on Galatians 6:14 ("Far be it from me to glory except in the cross of our Lord Jesus Christ") and asked those who wished to *recommit* their lives to Christ to raise their hands, all three hundred priests and nuns did so.[17]

> Lowell Berry, of Oakland, California, had *rededicated* his life to Christ in the Graham San Francisco crusade of 1958; previously a liberal churchman, he was president of the Northern California Council of Churches.[18]

Similarly, Pollock recounts in his official biography of Graham's crusades:

> Graham had officiated at weddings in Roman Catholic churches, but a few years earlier neither he, nor his Catholic hosts at Poznañ, nor the Baptists of Poland would have dreamed that he would conduct a mixed evangelistic crusade in a Catholic sanctuary anywhere in the world. . . . At the end, when Graham asked those who wished to decide for Christ to raise their hands, the response was prompt. Among the 200 or so who responded were twenty priests and some nuns, solemnly *rededicating* themselves to God.[19]

DOCTRINAL SIMPLIFICATION & PIETY AS A CRITERIA

This inclusivism on Graham's part has not gone without an acknowledged "simplification" of the gospel. To have sacramental churches and evangelical churches support and join behind a common message, a simplification of the message needs to occur. Doctrines that divide are laid aside as non-essentials. As he says, "Christians may disagree on minor issues and traditions. But they are united on one thing: the gospel of Jesus Christ."[20]

> I was reared in the Presbyterian church, but through a series of circumstances became a Baptist. Nevertheless, I do not go around the world proclaiming the Baptist faith, or the Presbyterian faith. I feel that as an evangelist I represent all the denominations and all the churches that are supporting the campaign. I try to avoid non-essentials issues that are not essential to salvation. Naturally, I proclaim the Gospel with boldness, and there are some churches that feel they cannot support such a campaign. . . . I also believe our identification with church leaders of many denominations has also contributed to a better understanding of the work of the evangelist and the work of the church.[21]

Furthermore, ten years into his evangelistic crusade ministry, he commented on some personal changes which are relevant in this discussion:

> A fourth change is to be seen in the fact that during the past ten years my concept of the church has taken on greater dimension. Ten years ago my concept of the church tended to be narrow and provincial, but after a decade of intimate contact with Christians the world over I am now aware that the family of God contains people of various ethnological, cultural, class and denominational differences. I have learned that there can even be minor disagreements of theology, methods and motives but that within the true church there is a mysterious unity that overrides all divisive factors.
> In groups which in my ignorant piousness I formerly "frowned upon" *I have found men so dedicated to Christ and so in love with the truth that I have felt unworthy to be in their presence.* I have learned that although Christians do not always agree, they can disagree agreeably, and that what is most needed in the church today is for us to show an unbelieving world that we love one another. To me the church has become a great, glorious and triumphant organism. It is the body of Christ, and the humblest member

> is an important part of that body. I have also come to believe
> that within every visible church there is a group of
> regenerated, dedicated disciples of Christ.[22]

In this scenario, where the content of the gospel is divested of any
matters that could cause division, *piety becomes a criteria* in judging
one's eternal state. As Graham says:

> I find many Christians who have grown up in Christian
> homes, been baptized or confirmed and had the benefit of
> Christian training, who are unaware of the time when they
> committed their lives to Christ, yet their faith and lives
> clearly testify that they know Christ.[23]

THE GOSPEL SIMPLIFIED AND ULTIMATELY REDEFINED

Invariably, as "nonessentials" are taken out, and as piety serves
as judge, a redefinition of the gospel follows. After all, declares Billy
Graham, what is important is that people make a commitment to
Christ.[24] The definition and the means of that commitment may vary.
A commitment through sacramental means, whereby grace is given
through baptism and other sacraments, is not excluded. As Dullea
had said earlier:

> In truth, he seems to want it both ways, both a
> once-and-for-all crisis-type decision that he presumes will
> remain fixed (aided of course by prayer and Bible reading),
> as well as a process-type conversion that is typified by
> nurture and gradual growth. Graham admits both kinds of
> conversion. On this point he is not a doctrinaire evan-
> gelical.[25]

We must understand that both concepts of conversions are inherently
linked to the respective theology of evangelicals and Catholics. The
evangelical "crisis-type" conversion, as it is called above, is
predicated on the biblical teaching that one must first believe that he
is totally lost and without hope (Mat. 9:12-13; cf. Eph. 2:1-3). He
can then become a child of God by faith alone in Christ's atoning

death and resurrection (John 1:12; Eph. 2:8; cf. I Cor. 15:1-3). In such a way, he can pass from death unto life (John 5:24).

In contrast, the Catholic "nurture" type of salvation is based on a rejection of the doctrine of faith alone.[26] Conversion to them begins with baptism which introduces one into the family of God. It is continued by the necessary demonstration of faith in Christ which takes the form of the practice and receiving of sacraments.[27] Graham's inclusivism consists of acknowledging both types of conversion. Graham does not really preach salvation by baptism or by works though, as we saw earlier, he does believe one can become a Christian through baptism. In general, he preaches salvation by faith. Evangelicals like that. However, what they have often missed is that it is not salvation by *biblical faith*, since *he leaves room for sacraments in his understanding of faith.* This subtle difference accommodates Catholics and other sacramental denominations. Ultimately, to Graham, salvation is through Christ, but it need not be through faith *alone*! Not only are the sacraments never repudiated, they are in fact at times endorsed (e.g. baptism, confirmation). **It is precisely at this point that** *the essence of the gospel is lost.*[28] Through his inclusivism, Graham's gospel has been redefined and faith alone has been in its very essence abandoned.

I would not want to suggest that no one has been born again at Graham's crusades. At times—in fact most often—Graham presents the "crisis-type" evangelical conversion. Yet, he will neither fully and biblically define salvation by faith *alone*, nor will he explain that faith is incompatible with a sacramental approach to salvation (since he does not believe it is). There may be some who hear the truths presented, who *ignore* the twisting of the gospel that inclusivism creates, who understand from the Bible that salvation is truly by faith alone, and who therefore *repudiate* any past trust in sacramental rituals to bring them into "relation" with God. It is these who can indeed become saved. No doubt, this has occurred over the years; but this is *in spite* of Graham's evangelical inclusive gospel, not because of it!

A STINGLESS MESSAGE

It is precisely because of this redefinition of the gospel, that Graham's message has no real sting in Catholic circles. Even from the very early days of Graham's ministry, Catholics have lent him their support, and they have done so increasingly over the decades.[29] There is no fear that Graham's crusades will sap the life of Catholic churches. In fact, Catholics in general trust Graham's crusades to bolster their churches. For instance, it has been reported:

> In St. Louis the official newspaper of the archdiocese gave unqualified support in a long editorial, saying, "Nothing but good can come from his crusades." It applauded his focus on "the person of Jesus the Savior who is both God and Man and on the sacred Scriptures which speak of him and his message. . . . If ever there was a time when all Christians should join together in giving witness to the beliefs they hold in common it is now."[30]

Catholics have encouraged their people to attend his crusades and are not afraid of his message.[31]   That is why they can write in their newspapers such things as:

> • What Catholics have in common with Billy Graham is shared conviction therefore about God, Jesus Christ and the Gospel as welcome and true news.[32]
> • When it comes to calling people to making a personal commitment to Jesus Christ, well, we really don't have any real differences. I think Catholics have a lot of trust in Dr. Graham and in his integrity.[33]

As one has said:

> Dr. Graham consistently promotes a deeper encounter between Jesus and the seeker. Graham never pretends that his way of evangelizing is the only way; he has both the humility and the experience to realize, however, that his gifts have been used by God to bring thousands to a new life.[34]

AS HE SAYS IT . . .

It is, therefore, not surprising, in light of Graham's embracing of inclusivism, to read some recent statements made by Graham in a personal interview with *Parade Magazine*:

> "I fully adhere to the fundamental tenets of the Christian faith for myself and my ministry," said the Rev. Billy Graham. "But, as an American, I respect other paths to God—and, as a Christian, I am called on to love them."[35]

Further in the interview, it is reported:

> Graham has been noted for his willingness to work with leaders of different religions. "Each time a President has asked me to lead the Inaugural prayer, I have argued that I should not do it alone, that leaders of other religions should be there too," he said. "We are a multireligious nation, and it would be good to reflect that at this important ceremonial occasion. I was only able to persuade Mr. Nixon."
>
> "We are all brothers and sisters in our hearts," he stressed. "We ought to love each other." What about other Christian leaders who do not share this view? "Well, I don't agree with them," Graham said.[36]

While it is tragic that any man would preach a gospel that is inclusive of both truth and error, it is devastating that so many evangelicals have not discerned the nature of Graham's message and beliefs. They, and the many others who need the unadulterated gospel of Christ, have only noticed the sheep's clothing (cf. Acts 20:39; 2 Cor. 11:13-14). Meanwhile, the wolf is free to carry on a very influential undermining of the gospel in evangelical circles.

BILLY GRAHAM'S INFLUENCE

As an influential leader in evangelicalism, Graham's inclusive gospel view has had great impact on the way many evangelicals perceive non-evangelicals within Christendom. They find new unity in the mutual profession of following Christ. However, they also give a decreasing significance to the details of how one comes to Christ. Though we cannot put sole responsibility on Graham for these changes, we can learn how Graham has been influential in turning the tide toward inclusivism.

THROUGH GRAHAM'S CRUSADES

From very early in his ministry, Graham has desired a wide support and representation of Christian churches. The ecumenical fruits from his efforts and from his crusades are not negligible. He himself has stated:

> I have seen that one of the great side-effects of our crusades is the way in which this common objective of evangelism brings Christians together. Sometimes they live in the same city but have never worked together before.[37]

He is not the only one to make such an observation. Pollock reports on Graham's visit to Poland:

> ... but it was the crusade's spirit of mutual cooperation for Christ which astonished and delighted Catholics, Protestants, and Orthodox alike. Working together to make the great evangelistic services a success, they discovered the depth of their brotherhood. As was said at the time, even the greatest Roman Catholic could not bring the Poles of different church loyalties together as equals, but Billy Graham could.[38]

Since the chasm between Catholics and evangelicals was so wide up until the 1940s, the process of tearing down that divide was not completed overnight. Over the years, through Graham's ecumenical policies and inclusive preaching, the work has progressed steadily. This is illustrated in the difference between the Twin-Cities crusades of 1973 and 1996:

> Planning for the crusade has crossed denominational lines, a development that excites local organizers. "During the 1973 Billy Graham crusade here, the Lutheran and Catholic

churches gave very little attention to the Graham crusade," Goold notes. "This time around it is very different, and we have received great enthusiasm and participation throughout the Lutheran and Catholic communities. . . ." Former Minnesota Gov. Al Quie, who chairs the local crusade committee, is also excited about the interdenominational cooperation brought about by the crusade. "I think to the extent we can get people across denominational lines and across ethnic lines to work together, it's especially beneficial," he notes. "Any time there's an excuse to work together I think it helps the whole spiritual climate. It's been amazing to me to see all the different people who volunteer to take part." "The Catholic leadership has gone all out, and been very involved. . . ."[39]

Therefore, what Billy Graham has accomplished more than any other, on a grass roots level, is an unparalleled contribution to the tearing down of the wall of division between evangelicals and non-evangelical sacramental denominations (Catholics, Anglicans, Eastern Orthodox, etc). But Graham's influence has been felt more than simply through his crusades. It has also had an impact through his legacies.

THROUGH GRAHAM'S LEGACIES

One of Graham's legacies is the popular magazine *Christianity Today*. It is no secret that Graham played a key role in the conception and beginning of the magazine.[40] Graham was instrumental in charting the course the magazine has taken and still remains the chairman of the Board of Directors. The magazine has had an irenic[41] and inclusive voice over the decades. It, too, has often pushed for an inclusive view of who is part of God's family within Christendom.[42] *Christianity Today*'s influence on the new spirit of ecumenical unity within Christendom cannot be underestimated.

Billy Graham has also been involved in the leadership of world congresses on evangelism.[43] From Berlin, to Lausanne, to Manila (called Lausanne II), one can observe the growth of inclusivism.

In 1966, Berlin led the way with a definite spirit of ecumenicalism, as Martin reports:

> In addition to these erstwhile heathen, the roster also included representatives from both the National and World Council of Churches, as well as from Roman Catholic and Jewish observers. It was, however, notably free of separatistic Fundamentalists, an omission that would not go unnoticed. To some, the experience of sitting at a common table with this ecumenical, international, and multi cultural mélange was enough to transform a simple meal into a foretaste of the messianic banquet.[44]

The Lausanne Congress of 1974 continued the trend toward evangelical inclusivism.[45] Many sessions and papers spoke in a positive tone of the Roman Catholic Church and other sacramental churches.[46]

But even more explicit was the last world congress, Lausanne II held in Manila in July 1989. The Manila Manifesto, a document signed by the evangelical participants, is a classic case of evangelical inclusivism:

> Our reference to "the whole church" is not a presumptuous claim that the universal church and the evangelical community are synonymous. For we recognize that there are many churches which are not part of the evangelical movement. Evangelical attitudes to the Roman Catholic and Orthodox Churches differ widely. Some evangelicals are praying, talking, studying Scripture and working with these churches. Others are strongly opposed to any form of dialogue or cooperation with them. All evangelicals are aware that serious theological differences between remain. Where appropriate, and so long as biblical truth is not compromised, cooperation may be possible in such areas as Bible translation, the study of contemporary theological and ethical issues, social work, and political action. We wish to make it clear, however, that common evangelism demands a common commitment to the gospel. . . . *We confess our own share of responsibility for the brokenness of the body of Christ*, which is a major stumbling block to world evangelization. We determine to go on seeking that unity in truth for which Christ prayed. We are persuaded that the

right way forward toward closer cooperation is frank and patient dialogue on the basis of the Bible with all who share our concerns. To this we gladly commit ourselves.[47]

The statement on first observation seems to be written as neutrally as possible. It admits a variety of attitudes and views within evangelicalism. It even affirms solidly that: " . . . common evangelism demands a common commitment to the gospel." But please notice the underlying premise of the statement which is found in the final paragraph. The phrase "the brokenness of the body" clearly expresses the premise of those who signed the manifesto: though divided, all parties mentioned (evangelicals, Roman Catholic, Orthodox Churches) are **all within the body of Christ**. It is upon this premise that they commit themselves to "patiently dialogue" in order to come to a greater unity.

Perhaps the most explicit case of an inclusive statement is seen in Tom Houston's address in one of the plenary sessions of Lausanne II. Tom Houston is the International Director of the Lausanne Committee for World Evangelism (LCWE), which was started to continue the work of the Lausanne Congress. Billy Graham is the honorary chairman and Leighton Ford is the chairman of this evangelical organization.[48] In his session, Houston spoke on unity:

> I was a separatist as a young pastor. Where two poles, I wanted to destroy or exclude the other pole. Then I realized God worked with magnetic poles, the North and the South, and they created a field of tension within which things could be done. . . .
>
> There are six saving acts of God in Jesus Christ. The first is the incarnation. The Word became a human being and lived among us. This is the controlling truth for Anglicans and Roman Catholics. They concentrate on the presence of Christ and emphasize continuity in the life of the people of God.
>
> The second saving act is the Cross, the Atonement. . . . The Lutherans and the Evangelicals center on the atonement. They concentrate on the pardon of Christ, emphasizing the discontinuity of conversion.
>
> The third saving act of God is the Resurrection. . . . This is the paramount truth for the Orthodox Churches. . . .

The fourth saving act is the Ascension. . . . This is the great truth for Presbyterians and the Reformed Churches. . . .

The fifth saving act is Pentecost, the sending of the Spirit. This is the central truth for the Pentecostals and Charismatics. . . .

The sixth saving act is yet to come. It is the Advent, the Second Coming of Christ. This is the theme of the Seventh Day and other Adventists. . . .

Now all these churches believe in all these six saving acts, but they emphasize one and seem to attract people whose need is met by one. Ideally we should all emphasize all, but no one group is all of these to tell and show the whole gospel. And there are tensions between them. . . . The Incarnation people emphasize the gradual growth of the Christian life beginning in baptism, often in infancy. Those who preach the Cross are impatient with that and pursue the discontinuity of dramatic conversion. But both are necessary.

God gives us each a torch to carry, but it is one procession. We do not need to apologize for our torch. Carry it high but let us not imagine it is whole truth. Let us affirm the whole procession and the others in it. . . . Let us make our unflinching goal to stay together under the banner of the Word of God as reflected in the Lausanne Covenant and show the world the fullness of the saving acts of God in Christ.[49]

Even a casual reading of I Corinthians 15:1-4 will reveal the great heresy of the above address. In fact, I would even refrain from calling the above a case of *evangelical* inclusivism—it is inclusive for sure, but there is nothing really evangelical in Houston's message.

Yet in all my reading concerning Lausanne II, nothing was found that addressed the error of Houston's understanding.[50] At the same time, most of the Manila Manifesto is biblically sound concerning the gospel.[51] How can avowed evangelicals who participated at Lausanne II accept Tom Houston's view of the gospel? The answer is found in the paradox and subtlety of evangelical inclusivism.

CONCLUSION

Billy Graham has had much "fruit" for his labor. Even from a casual knowledge of his ministry and his preaching, one cannot miss his advancement of a more unified ecumenical global church. This ecumenism is based on the inclusive gospel which he has embraced and which he has been propagating for decades, whether through his crusades or through the institutions he has set up. His biggest influence on evangelicalism as a whole is to have substantially brought down the wall which once distinguished genuine believers from those who are trusting in their sacramental faith to get them to God. As this wall is taken down, the greater "unity" being formed is based on an inclusive gospel. This gospel is invariably a redefined and simplified gospel. It is not the gospel of Jesus Christ, which is exclusive, absolute and through faith alone.

The very fact that Graham has preached an inclusive gospel has caused great confusion in the ranks of the faithful. Even most who oppose Graham's ministry have missed the real issue. The issue goes far beyond the problem of a lack of separation. It deals with the very basics of the gospel. Some, and maybe even much of what Graham says is biblically accurate. But when you hear him through, his message as a whole turns you away from the gospel of Jesus Christ unto another message . . . the stingless message of evangelical inclusivism.

NOTES ON CHAPTER 2

1. "Catholics Laud 'Dr. Graham,' " *Christianity Today* (December 8, 1967): 41-42.

2. William Martin, A Prophet with Honor (New York: William Morrow and Company, Inc., 1991), 222-223.

3. Ibid., 220.

4. Ibid., 294. Martin also reflects on Graham's attitude toward the WCC when he reports:

    > He attended the World Council's meetings, rejoiced in the fellowship of renowned ecclesiastics, even when they singled him out for criticism, and "thrilled at the whole process of seeing world churchmen sitting down together, praying together, discussing together." Even so, he felt their attitude toward evangelism was a grievous error [327].

    Regarding Graham's rapprochement to Roman Catholicism, I will refer the reader to Ian Paisley's book, Billy Graham and the Church of Rome (Greenville, SC: Bob Jones University Press, 1970). See also Martin, A Prophet with Honor; John Pollock, Billy Graham: Evangelist to the World (Minneapolis: World Wide Publications, 1979).

5. This could be understood from some statements Graham has made. As Pollock says:

    > Graham rejects the view that "because we have people on the committee from liberal institutions we are endorsing the theology of those institutions. The theology we endorse is the theology I will be proclaiming from the platform. If they want to come and endorse what I am saying, thank God! . . . I will never go anywhere where there are strings on my message. I ask all to attend and cooperate who wish to, regardless of what identification they may have. Who serves on what committee seems to be rather incidental. It is what is proclaimed from the platform that counts" [Pollock, 112].

    However, this does not take away the fact that from the pulpit Graham has given spiritual recognition to renowned liberals and to orthodox Catholics. It will also be shown in the remaining part of this chapter that Graham has *from the platform* made clear what theology he holds to, and that, through his inclusivism, he has made room for liberals or Catholics within the Christian family at large, though substantial differences in theology are recognized. This does not deny that he attempts to "win" them. As will also be shown, he often sees this "winning" them as a rededication to Christ, not necessarily as a totally new Christian experience.

6. "Catholics Laud 'Dr. Graham,' " *Christianity Today* (December 8, 1967): 41-42. Graham said of that occasion: "And the first degree I got from a Catholic institution, Belmont Abbey, I was honored" [Martin, 601].

7. Some North American evangelicals make a great distinction between American Catholicism and Roman Catholicism.

8. Quoted by Martin [460-461, emphasis added]. Martin goes on to talk of Wilson, Graham's closest associate:

> In a similar vein, T. W. Wilson observed that television evangelist Jimmy Swaggart was "absolutely wrong" in his insistence that Catholics are not Christians in the eyes of God. "A number of doctrines they teach," Wilson said, "we don't subscribe to, nor would we ever. But to say that they are not Christians—man alive! Anybody that receives Jesus Christ as their Lord and Savior is converted! They're born again! I believe the pope is a converted man. I believe a lot of these wonderful Catholics are Christians. I'd like to shake them and turn them around and tell them, 'You don't need all this. You don't need to go to the confession booth and confess all your sins to that priest. He's just a man.' So there are differences, but that doesn't mean they're not converted" [Martin, 460-461].

9. See the Pope John Paul II's book, <u>A Millenial Hope? Crossing the Threshold of Hope</u>, ed. Vittorio Messori (New York: Knopf, 1994).

10. Horton, in his foreword of <u>Faith Alone</u> by R.C. Sproul, 11.

11. Billy Graham, "Conversion—A Personal Revolution," *The Ecumenical Review* (July, 1967): 277-278, emphasis added.

12. Quoted from the *Lutheran Standard*, October 27, 1961, by David W. Cloud <dcloud@whidbey.net> *Billy Graham's Disobedience To The Word of God.* Internet WWW page, at URL: <http://cnview.com/on_line_resources/billy_grahams_disobedience.htm> (version current 6 Nov 1997).

13. Carolo W. Dullea, <u>W. F. 'Billy' Graham's 'Decision for Christ,' A Study in Conversion</u> (Rome: Typis Pontificiae Universitatis Gregorianae, 1971), 60. Graham gave an interview, which reports:

> When people come forward, have they truly let Christ and love into their hearts? And is that enough? "No, it isn't enough," he said. "It's a beginning. Love does not suddenly come full-blown and fill people up. They have to commit themselves to prayer and service in order to keep love growing in their hearts" [Collin Greer, " 'Our Task Is To Do All We Can—Not To Sit And Wait,' " *Parade Magazine* (October 20, 1996): 5].

14. J. Baille, <u>Baptism and Conversion</u> (London: n.p., 1964), 49, 95-108. Note: the author, J. Baille, quotes another person named John Baillie.

15. Dullea, 97-99, emphasis added.

16. Billy Graham, "Loneliness," Personal recording at the Twin Cities Billy Graham Crusade of 1996, June 19, 1996, emphasis added.

17. Martin, 490, emphasis added. The following excerpt from a Catholic's point of view illustrates how Catholics can absorb the "new birth" experience into their whole theology and consider it only as a rededication:

> In Warsaw Graham spoke to an overflow crowd of nearly 1,000 and led an evangelism workshop for more than 450 clergy and other religious workers,

including several Catholic seminary professors and teaching nuns. From that beginning visible signs of ecumenical warmings, in a climate Protestant leaders typically described as unfriendly, accompanied Graham's appearances. At Warsaw's Catholic seminary, the dean of theology introduced Graham by recalling how, during a sojourn in Chicago a few years earlier, a black woman on a bus had asked him if he was saved. He had responded, "Can't you see my collar?" The woman, a Baptist, had been unimpressed. "I don't care about that," she had said. "Have you been born again?" The dean related that, stunned by this challenge, he had gone back to his room, read the third chapter of John once again, and had a new experience of Christ that led him to rededicate his life. He was grateful to Baptists, he said, and he welcomed the most famous Baptist of all to Poland" [Martin, 489-90].

Beyond being a "convert" and staying in the Catholic Church, consider the following: "As Billy entered the hall, a Catholic priest ran up and shook him warmly by the hand, saying he was in the priesthood because of hearing him at a crusade" [Pollock, 100].

18. Pollock, 131.

19. Pollock, 310-311, emphasis added. Martin says of that Poznań occasion, "Graham's first sermon ever in a Catholic church occurred at Poznań in western Poland, where he prayed that the Holy Spirit would unite the hearts of the Roman Catholics and Protestants worshiping together on that occasion . . . " [Martin, 490].

20. Graham, "A Biblical Standard for Evangelists," 125.

21. Ibid., 106-107.

22. Graham, "What Ten Years Have Taught Me," *The Christian Century* (February 17, 1960): 187-188.

23. Graham, "Conversion," 279.

24. As Graham says, "After all," he explained, "I have no quarrel with the Catholic Church. Christians are not limited to any church. The only question is: are you committed to Christ?" [Martin, 222-223].

25. Dullea, 97-99.

26. This is explicitly illustrated in a statement by Catholic editor, Richard Neuhaus:

> The *Catechism of the Catholic Church* does not reject the distinctive Reformation formula that justification is by grace alone through faith alone because of Christ alone. Neither does it affirm it. To address it at all would require going on to make clear that grace is not alone but confirms human freedom, that living faith is not alone but issues in a life of obedience, that Christ is not alone but always to be found in the company of His Church [Richard Neuhaus, "Protestant Reformation and Universal Church," *First Things* (March 1995): 70].

27. Rahner, a Catholic, discusses conversion:

> The Catholic approaches this basic decision (option fondamentale) in a different way from the evangelical. For him, his orientation generally takes place at his

Baptism, without his even being aware of it. He is generally brought up in some kind of Christian nurture, adequate or inadequate as it may be. When he reaches adulthood he must in a conscious, mature, fully human way acknowledge, ratify, "appropriate," i.e. make his very own, this option. This usually is done in repeated acts of more or less intensity and with more or less self-awareness: in First Communion, in Confirmation, frequent Mass, Communion, confession, in prayer and spiritual reading, especially of the Scriptures, in times of missions and retreats. The emphasis is on repeated acts, the formation of habits, organic growth [K. Rahner, "Conversion," in *Sacramentum Mundi*, Vol. 2, pp. 5-6].

Rahner also calls attention to the importance of Catholics making the kind of decision Graham preaches:

Pastoral practice and theology, however, ought not to overlook the phenomenon of conversion as a decisive function of pastoral care of the individual. Not only because freedom in the sense of man's unique, historical self-realization intended to be final in regard to God, implies a fundamental decision (option fondamentale), but also because a decision of this kind ought to be carried out as constitutive of man's very essence. From this point of view, conversion is not so much or always a turning away from definite particular sins of the past, as a resolute, radical and radically conscious, personal and in each instance unique adoption of Christian life. And in this, freedom, decision as absolutely final, and grace are really experienced (cf., e.g., Gal. 3:5) [sic]. Furthermore, in a society which in philosophical outlook is extremely heterogeneous and anti-Christian, Christianity in the individual, deprived of support from the milieu, cannot survive in the long run without a conversion of this kind, i.e., personal fundamental choice of faith and Christian life" [Ibid.].

Even Keith Fournier, who calls himself an evangelical Catholic Christian, confirms the Catholic rejection of a one-time conversion/death-unto-life type of conversion:

What makes me a *Catholic* Christian? First, I am a Catholic Christian who can point to various times of conversion in my life, "evangelical moments" as I call them. This is consonant with my understanding of conversion . . ." [Keith Fournier, Evangelical Catholics (Nashville: Thomas Nelson Publishers, 1990), 17].

He has also admitted his need of deeper conversions.

28. For a good discussion on this subject, see R.C. Sproul, Faith Alone (Grand Rapids: Baker Books, 1995).

29. Martin reports on early Catholic ecumenical backing of Graham:

Cardinal Cushing had looked on Graham with favor. During the 1950 campaign, he had written an editorial entitled "Bravo, Billy!" for the diocesan newspaper. Just before the 1964 crusade got under way, he sounded another approving note by announcing that the crusade would "surely be of great importance for many Christians in the Greater Boston area," and assuring Graham that he and other Catholics would be praying for God's blessing on him in the expectation that he would "lead many to the knowledge of Our Lord." Because Cushing flew off to attend the Second Vatican Council in Rome immediately after making that statement, the two men did not meet during the crusade's first phase, but Graham made a point of stressing his own "tremendous admiration" for the cardinal.
. . . [At a forty-five-minute televised conversation], the cardinal, dressed in street clothes rather than in the ornate robes of his office, generously declared that "I have never known of a religious crusade that was more effective" than Graham's and assured the evangelist and his supporters that "although we Catholics do not join with them in body, yet in spirit and heart we unite with them in praying God's blessing upon this Christian and Christlike experience in our community." He

urged Catholic young people to attend the crusade services with no fear of disloyalty to their church, assuring them that Graham's message "is one of Christ crucified, and no Catholic can do anything but become a better Catholic from hearing him. . . . I'm one hundred percent for Dr. Graham. He is extraordinarily gifted. The hand of God must be upon him." . . . Never one to be outcomplimented, Graham professed to regard his new friend as "the leading ecumenist in America," lavished further praise on Pope John XXIII and his recent successor, Paul VI and heralded Vatican II as a major step in dissipating the clouds of resentment and mistrust that had separated Catholics and Protestants. . . .

While most observers either praised or paid little attention to the conversation, some in both camps showed discomfort at its amicable spirit. . . . But both men had meant what they said, leading Graham to observe that in contrast to the rancor and suspicion that attended the 1960 election, "this is sort of a new day." The encounter thus stands as a significant marker on the course that Graham steadfastly chose to follow, a course that led him from the narrow confines of the strictest sort of sectarianism to the open ground upon which one is reluctant to deny anyone the right to be called, if not brother, at least neighbor [Martin, 309-310].

30. Pollock, 130.

31. Bob Moran , "Crusade won't raid Catholic flock, Paulist says," *The Catholic Times*, (April 1990): 11; Peter V. Conley "Catholics and the Billy Graham Hub Crusade," *The Pilot* (May 11, 1982); Terry Mattingly "Catholic Counselors Help Brethern Heed Graham Call," *Rocky Mount News* (July 25, 1987).

32. Moran, 11.

33. Mattingly, "Catholics counselors help brethren heed Graham call."

34. Ibid.

35. Collin Greer, " 'Our Task Is To Do All We Can—Not To Sit And Wait,' " *Parade Magazine* (October 20, 1996): 4-6.

36. Ibid.

37. Billy Graham, <u>A Biblical Standard for Evangelists</u> (Minneapolis: World Wide Publications, 1984), 126.

38. Pollock, 310.

39. Doug Trouten, "Graham comes to Metrodome" in the *Minnesota Christian Chronicle* (Special Edition: Greater Twin Cities Billy Graham Crusade Edition. n.d.): 1-2.

40. Martin, 211-216.

41. "Conducive to or operating toward peace or conciliation" (Webster's).

42. E.g. Thomas F. Stransky, "Catholics and Evangelicals: a Roman Priest Looks across the Divide," *CT* (October 22, 1982): 28-30; Kenneth Kantzer, "Reflections: Five Years of Change," *CT* (November 26, 1982): 14-20; James P. Degnan, "The Nonsense of Liberal Catholics," *CT* (November 21, 1969): 3-

6; Marshall Shelley, "What Catholics and Evangelicals have in common," *CT* (November 26, 1982): 66; What Separates Evangelicals and Catholics," *CT* (October 23, 1981): 12-15; John R. W. Stott, "Evangelicals and Roman Catholics" *CT* (August 12, 1977): 30-31; Francis Wilkerson, "Evangelicals and Anglo-Catholics," *CT* (January 5, 1962): 9-10; Howard Zehr, "Peril Swelling Ranks of Sudanese Christians," *CT* (April 4, 1994): 80-81; Jim Reapsome, "What China Doesn't Need," *CT* (May 16, 1994): 17; etc. These articles and news reports vary in degree of inclusivism.

43. Martin, 442; see also Leighton Ford, "Proclaim Christ" in Proclaim Christ until He Come, ed., J. D. Douglas (Minneapolis: World Wide Publications, 1990), 50.

44. Martin, 328; see also 338-339.

45. The conference was clearly an evangelical conference. Its delegates were chosen as such, and its confession of faith is clearly evangelical [J. D. Douglas, ed. Let The Earth Hear His Voice International Congress on World Evangelization [Lauzanne, Switzerland] (Minneapolis: World Wide Publications, 1975) 27, 3-9].

46. One interesting section of a paper presented at Lausanne goes as follows:
    Development of a consistent view of Christian experience. Many believing Catholics are puzzled by the evangelical Protestants' over-emphasis on the *experience* of conversion, and their under-emphasis on the *fruits* of conversion. Some Protestants may need to examine their own view of Christian experience as they increasingly meet Catholic believers who have not had dramatic conversion experiences and yet evidently manifest the fruits of the Spirit. Evangelical Protestants who are critical of the emphasis on experience in the Catholic Charismatic movement, should consider being also critical of their own emphasis on experience in conversion. The biblical criteria for assessing the spiritual life of a person do not seem to depend on the *way in which* a person was either converted or sanctified, but rather on the results of that "experience." "By their fruits ye shall know them" is a test which can be equally applied to evangelical Protestants and Roman Catholics. When all is said and done, what the world looks for in Christians is a practical and demonstrable evidence of the inner knowledge of God which they claim to have. It was a Catholic, Cardinal Suhard, who said that to be a witness is not to engage in propaganda or always to try to convince others that our way is the right one, but rather "to live in such a way, that our lives would not make sense if God did not exist!" AMEN [Ramez L. Atallah, "Some Trends in the Roman Catholic Church Today," in Let the World Hear His Voice, 882].

Furthermore, the response by the evangelical participants to another paper on Catholic trends reveals a great degree of inclusivism:
    In direct response to the paper, a deep sense of thankfulness was expressed for the new openness of the Roman church. The group did, however, *doubt* the proposition that the leadership of the church was in the hands of the progressives. Some felt that the changes were more apparent than real and that the historic mistrust of the Roman church was still justified. There was *unconditional* approval of meeting with Roman Catholics for Bible study, sharing Christian experience, and praying together" ["Evangelization among Nominal or Sacramentalist Christians Report," 883].

Notably, throughout the conference, sessions speakers gave the idea that the problem plaguing Christendom was "Nominalism," whether it be in

Protestantism, Roman Catholicism or in the Eastern Orthodox Church [883-884]. Nowhere was it said that the main problem with the Roman Catholic Church and the Orthodox Church is not nominalism but simply apostasy from the faith.

47. "Manila Manifesto," *World Evangelism* (Special Congress Report, n.d.): 35, emphasis added [also in Proclaim Christ Until He Comes]. Fruit of the conference can be seen in Pollock's report:

> All Christendom had become aware once again of the integrity and importance of a Biblical theology of evangelization, of its practical implications, and especially of the vigor of theological and evangelistic leadership emerging from the so-called Third World. Some dozen regional or national congresses on world evangelization, and smaller seminars, had been planned and coordinated. A nine-day seminar for Papua (New Guinea) in June 1976 had included Roman Catholics, one of whom remarked, "It was unthinkable as little as two years ago." A factor leading to this, other than Lausanne, was the crusade tour four years before by Billy Graham's black associate, Ralph Bell, strongly supported by the Roman Catholic archbishop as well as by all Protestant churches [Pollock, 252].

48. This was the situation in 1990. Later developments are unknown. Regarding the organization being evangelical, Covell says:

> ". . . Fundamentalists, conservative evangelicals, and ecumenical evangelicals. The latter two groups can be identified, at least informally, with the Lausanne Committee for World Evangelization (LCWE) and its doctrinal and mission commitment. American evangelicals associated with the LCWE come largely from particular evangelical denominations belonging to the National Associations of Evangelicals or from interdenominational churches [Ralph R. Covell, "The Christian Gospel and World Religions: How much Have American Evangelicals Changed?" *International Bulletin of Missionary Research* (January 1991): 12; see also Kenneth Kantzer, "Reflections: Five years of Change," *Christianity Today* (November 26, 1982): 17-18].

49. Tom Houston, "Let's Stay Together," *World Evangelism* (November-December 1989/January 1990): 8; also found in "LCWE's Goals for the Future" by Tom Houston, in Proclaim Christ Until He Comes, 370-371.

50. This is not to say that no one did expose Houston's error. However, it apparently did not create much of a negative reaction, nor did any public criticism transpire in the official papers and report on the Congress [See Proclaim Christ Until He Comes].

51. "The Manila Manifesto," *World Evangelism* (Special Congress Report, n.d.): 35.

Chapter 3

THE CONTINUING TREND
-- DEVELOPMENTS ON THE EVANGELICAL SCENE

One swallow does not make a summer; nor does one trickle, or a set of trickles, make a river; but it is worth noting here that mission ventures involving evangelicals and Catholics side by side not only in social witness but also in evangelism and nurture have already begun to appear. Billy Graham's cooperative evangelism, in which all churches of an area are invited to share, is one such. Charismatic gatherings where the distinction between Protestant and Catholic vanishes in a Christ-centered unity of worship, fellowship and joy, are a further example. Could it be that ECT [Evangelicals and Catholics Together] is fuel for a fire that is already alight?
— J. I. Packer[1]

IN 1985, in New England, a Baptist pastor I knew presented a booth at Congress '85, a regional congress on evangelism organized by the Evangelistic Association of New England (EANE). His booth's theme was how to witness to Roman Catholics. He displayed Roman Catholic literature to expose their beliefs as well as other literature on how to lead Roman Catholics to the Lord. Great, right? Not according to many at the Congress. The booth caused a major scene toward the end of the week. The local priests came and spoke against the booth. This raised quite a stir until the organizers of the Congress came and made the pastor remove the "divisive" literature. The next day, a Roman Catholic priest spoke in one of the Congress' plenary sessions and received a great welcome by the leaders and the audience.[2]

I would like to hope that the above was an isolated event. However, in light of many developments in recent years, it hardly seems to be the case. Key leaders and popular organizations within the evangelical movement are turning to an inclusivism which has not left the gospel unaffected.

So far, I have presented evangelical inclusivism as it relates only to those within Christendom who profess to know Christ. Another form of evangelical inclusivism is surfacing on the current scene—an inclusivism which relates to those who have never heard of Jesus Christ.[3]

THE INCLUSION OF THOSE WHO HAVE NEVER HEARD

In the report given of *The Evangelical-Roman Catholic Dialogue on Mission, 1977-1984* (ERCDOM), it is said:

> Evangelicals insist, however, that according to the New Testament those outside Christ are 'perishing', and that they can receive salvation only in and through Christ. . . . Most Evangelicals believe that, because they reject the light they have received, they condemn themselves to hell. Many are reluctant to pronounce on their destiny, have no wish to limit the sovereignty of God, and prefer to leave this issue to him. Others go further in expressing their openness to the possibility that God may save some who have not heard of Christ, but immediately add that, if he does so, it will not be because of their religion, sincerity or actions (there is no possibility of salvation by good works), but only because of his grace freely given on the ground of the atoning death of Christ.[4]

This openness is being suggested in many evangelical works and articles.[5] Some authors show an uncertainty on the matter. They believe God's eternal power and deity are revealed through nature, but that nature's witness (general revelation) is not sufficient unto salvation.[6] Even so they go on to ask: *"Must faith in Jesus Christ which is a necessary response to God's offer of salvation always be explicit?"*[7] And so they leave the door open to the possibility of asking, "Could it be that those to whom God has uniquely revealed himself as Savior, but without revealing his name, be saved, if they have responded by casting themselves wholly in repentance and faith upon the God of whom they are dimly aware?"[8]

Other than the fact that the plain teaching of Acts 4:12, Romans 9:14-16 and 10:17 is ignored, the greatest problem of this kind of inclusivism is that it tends to redefine the gospel. This is most obvious in Millard Erickson's writings:

> Perhaps, in other words, it is possible to receive the benefit of Christ's death without conscious knowledge-belief in the name of Jesus. What, then, is the essential nature of the gospel message? Several elements are involved: (1) The belief in one good powerful God. (2) The belief that he (man) owes this God perfect obedience to his law. (3) The consciousness that he does not meet this standard, and therefore is guilty and condemned. (4) The belief that God is merciful, and will forgive and accept those who cast themselves upon his mercy.[9]

Erickson's four essential elements of the gospel message are far from those given in the Word of God by the mouth of the apostle Paul! 1 Corinthians 15 is very explicit on what constitutes the gospel. It is the death of Christ for our sins and His resurrection from the dead. Genuine belief is necessary for one to be saved (1 Cor. 15:2). The "essential nature of the gospel" as set forth above by Erickson is a gospel which is void of any real biblical essence. We will deal with these issues in greater detail in Chapter 5.[10]

This gospel-redefined inclusivism is not the majority view in evangelicalism, but it certainly is a growing view, as James Hunter documents in his book, <u>Evangelicalism: The Coming Generation</u>. He shows the shift that is occurring in evangelicalism in its understanding of salvation and Christ's exclusivity. This is manifest, according to Hunter, in a growing reticence to declare as lost either those who have never heard the gospel, or those who have shown exceptional Christian virtues in their lives (e.g., Gandhi).[11] This trend in evangelicalism is what permits Hunter to conclude: "The meaning of such doctrines as the inerrancy/infallibility of Scripture, the justification through Christ *alone* . . . has become more *inclusive*."[12]

THE INCLUSION OF THOSE
WHO HOLD TO "ANOTHER" GOSPEL

The Reformation was a movement which denounced the errors and spiritual darkness of the Roman Catholic Church. However, today many evangelicals are claiming to find more light than darkness in Roman Catholicism. The traditional evangelical understanding that Roman Catholicism is apostate Christianity is often being undermined, repudiated, and even attacked within evangelical circles. In an era which some have called the Ecumenical Age,[13] the widespread focus within Christendom has been on the unity of the Church, a focus which has also often been seen within evangelicalism.

Charles Colson, a noted evangelical leader, has written explicitly on this subject in his book, The Body. He holds to the unity of the body, a body which, according to him, would include for instance Catholics, Anglicans, Lutherans, and Protestants. For example, to him, Mother Theresa had a genuine faith and devotion to God.[14] In fact, he very pointedly says that the gospel she had is the gospel.[15] He also says:

> The fact is, we can learn from one another. Personally, while I've formed strong doctrinal convictions, I've been enriched deeply by my fellowship with those who hold different, but equally strong doctrinal convictions—particularly my Catholic, Anglican, Orthodox, and Lutheran brothers and sisters.[16]

As alarming as his view is, the realization of the wide support he received from other major evangelical leaders (J. I. Packer, Dr. Jerry Falwell, Carl F. H. Henry, to name a few) makes it even more so.[17]

This trend toward ecumenism and inclusivism within evangelicalism is not only toward Roman Catholicism, but also toward others, such as liberals. For instance, the trend is leading many evangelicals to seek closer ties with the World Council of Churches.[18]

> As in Vancouver eight years ago, the evangelicals in Canberra issued their own statement at the end of WCC's meetings. But unlike earlier evangelical statements, its tone was chiefly cooperative. It acknowledged some continuing differences with the WCC but expressed appreciation for the opportunity to participate in the assembly. "The experience provided by the assembly of work in subsections enabled evangelicals and those from other perspectives to discover each other *not as antagonists but as believers together.* In particular we recognized many common theological commitments and concerns with the Orthodox," their published statement declared.[19]

This trend is not new, as it has been seen with Billy Graham for some time now, but it appears to have become more explicit and more wide spread. In an article in the *Evangelical Quarterly*, Tony Lane expresses very clearly the contention of the inclusivists:

> We must beware of the attitude that will acknowledge no-one as a true Christian who does not express their faith in evangelical terms. Can it not be that many Roman Catholics come to a living personal faith which then expresses itself through the available channels of catholic piety?[20]

In his article, Lane goes on to state that he regards Catholics as "separated brethren."[21]

We know biblically from Ephesians 4:4-6 that the Church is one. Furthermore, from Ephesians 5:23 and Colossians 1:24 we are told that the Church is the body of Christ. Therefore to focus on the unity of the Church is not necessarily wrong. However, when this focus includes as part of the Church those who were previously considered outside genuine Christianity, some great questions and issues arise. What is essential Christianity? What makes one a Christian?

Furthermore, regarding the above questions, I would also like to point out that the issues brought up in today's ecumenical trends do not relate solely to personal and/or ecclesiastical separation. They go far beyond. It is one thing to seek closer ties with "apostates"—and I am not justifying it—but it is a totally different one to see these apostates as believers![22] It is the definition of the gospel that is at stake.

"Evangelicals And Catholics Together"

The most significant development in the matter of evangelical inclusivism is the drafting of the document, "Evangelicals & Catholics Together: The Christian Mission in the Third Millennium" (hereafter, ECT). To this document, I will give most of my attention, since much of what has been said recently within evangelicalism relates to this statement. ECT was issued as an unofficial document in the spring of 1994 and calls on "evangelicals and Catholics to recognize each other as Christians. . . ."[23] Though it was unofficial, it must not be thought that the Catholics involved were acting totally independently from Rome. The Catholic leader of the accord, Neuhaus, said "that the 'appropriate parties at the Holy See' gave the effort their 'strongest encouragement.' "[24] On the evangelical side, though it was unofficial, it did represent some very notable evangelical leaders and theologians such as Chuck Colson (leader), Bill Bright of Campus Crusade, J. I. Packer, Pat Robertson, Os Guiness, and others.

The statement spells out clearly the basis upon which Catholics and evangelicals can cooperate in the war against secularism. It begins by saying:

> We are Evangelical Protestants and Roman Catholics who have been led through prayer, study, and discussion to common convictions about Christian faith and mission. . . .
> As Christ is one, so the Christian mission is one. That one mission can be and should be advanced in diverse ways. Legitimate diversity, however, should not be confused with existing divisions between Christians that obscure the one Christ and hinder the one mission. There is a necessary connection between the visible unity of Christians and the mission of the one Christ. We together pray for the fulfillment of the prayer of Our Lord: "May they all be one." . . .
> The one Christ and one mission includes many other Christians, notably the Eastern Orthodox and those Protestants not commonly identified as Evangelical. All

Christians are encompassed in the prayer, "May they all be one." . . .

We affirm together that we are justified by grace through faith because of Christ. . . .

All who accept Christ as Lord and Savior are brothers and sisters in Christ. Evangelicals and Catholics are brothers and sisters in Christ. . . . However imperfect our communion with one another, we recognize that there is but one Christ and the church is his body. However difficult the way, we recognize that we are called by God to a fuller realization of our unity in the body of Christ. The only unity to which we would give expression is unity in the truth, and the truth is this: "There is one body and one Spirit, just as you were called to the one hope that belongs to your call, one Lord, one faith, one baptism, one God and Father of us all, who is above all and through all and in all . . . " (Ephesians 4).[25]

It is interesting that the "one truth" mentioned is the truth concerning unity—that both parties *are* genuinely Christian (*one in Christ*). However, it is obvious from reading the rest of the document that other truths, such as the biblical truth concerning conversion, baptism, faith, or regeneration—matters which relate to *how* one becomes a Christian—could not be used to unite both parties, since a wide divergence on those issues are acknowledged.

We do not presume to suggest that we can resolve the deep and long-standing differences between Evangelicals and Catholics. . . .

We note some of the differences and disagreements that must be addressed more fully and candidly in order to strengthen between us a relationship of trust in obedience to truth. Among points of difference in doctrine, worship, practice, and piety that are frequently thought to divide us are these:

• The church as an integral part of the Gospel or the church as a communal consequence of the Gospel.

• The church as visible communion or invisible fellowship of true believers.

• The sole authority of Scriptures (*sola scriptura*) or Scripture as authoritatively interpreted in the church.

• The "soul freedom" of the individual Christian or the Magisterium (teaching authority) of the community.

- The church as local congregation or universal communion.
- Ministry ordered in apostolic succession or the priesthood of all believers.
- Sacraments and ordinances as symbols of grace or means of grace.
- The Lord's Supper as eucharist sacrifice or memorial meal.
- Remembrance of Mary and the saints or devotion to Mary and the saints.
- Baptism as sacrament of regeneration or testimony to regeneration.[26]

Many of the points of disagreement mentioned above deal specifically with what makes one a Christian, or a recipient of God's grace (i.e. "sacraments . . . as symbol . . . or *means* of grace"; "Baptism as *sacrament . . .* or testimony . . . "). *How can both parties fundamentally consider each other within the body of Christ, when neither party agrees on what gets one into the body of Christ?* Sadly enough, however, such a question seems *irrelevant* to the inclusivist. In fact, the statement goes on to elaborate the clear differences regarding baptism and the new birth:

> In considering the many corruptions of Christian witness, we, Evangelicals and Catholics, confess that we have sinned against one another and against God. . . .
> Repentance and amendment of life do not dissolve remaining differences between us. In the context of evangelization and "reevangelization," we encounter a major difference in our understanding of the relationship between baptism and the new birth in Christ. *For Catholics, all who are validly baptized are born again and are truly, however imperfectly, in communion with Christ.* That baptismal grace is to be continuingly reawakened and revivified through conversion. For most Evangelicals, but not all, the experience of conversion is to be followed by baptism as a sign of new birth. For Catholics, all the baptized are already members of the church, however dormant their faith and life; for many Evangelicals, the new birth requires baptismal initiation into the community of the born again. These differing beliefs about the relationship between baptism, new birth, and membership in the church should be honestly

presented to the Christian who has undergone conversion. But again, his decision regarding communal allegiance and participation must be assiduously respected.

There are, then, differences between us that cannot be resolved here. But on this we are resolved: All authentic witness must be aimed at conversion to God in Christ by the power of the Spirit. Those converted—*whether understood as having received the new birth for the first time or as having experienced the reawakening of the new birth originally bestowed in the sacrament of baptism*—must be given full freedom and respect as they discern and decide the community in which they will live *their new life in Christ.*[27]

In the above, there is an alarming paradox: *conversion is what is mutually sought after, though both groups are admittedly in opposition as to their understanding of conversion.*

To the Catholic, new birth occurs at baptism and conversion can simply be a reawakening of that new birth. This type of new birth and conversion is diametrically contrary to any historical evangelical declaration of faith. Even the evangelicals who signed the document explicitly stated their differences with Rome in regards to their view of new birth. However, these same evangelicals, along with their Catholic co-signatories, are unmistakably inclusive. Both ways of conversion, either the renewal of the Catholics' new birth at infant baptism, or the evangelicals' new birth at conversion, are explicitly said to evidence "new life in Christ." So then to these evangelical inclusivists, it does not matter how you get converted, or what you believe about new birth and conversion. You can still be a genuine child of God.

Some have suggested that the document was drafted for political reasons, but suggesting this misses the foundational premise of the document. Even Richard Neuhaus, a Catholic signer of the document, said, "By far, the document's most important single statement . . . is the affirmation that evangelicals and Catholics are brothers and sisters in Christ. Everything else flows from that."[28]

Evangelical reactions to the documents ranged anywhere from strong opposition[29] to endorsement[30] and any where in between.[31]

ECT CLARIFICATION STATEMENT:
GREATER INCLUSIVISM YET!

It is hard to imagine getting more evangelically inclusive than that which was demonstrated with ECT. Yet this is what has occurred in the aftermath of ECT. How is one "more evangelically inclusive"? By affirming with even greater precision the evangelical faith, while still maintaining an inclusive view of the gospel.

Because of the negative reactions to the original document, Chuck Colson and other signatories of ECT drew up a clarification (here after referred to as the *Clarification*) in January 1995, at Fort Lauderdale. It stated:

1. Our para-church cooperation with evangelically committed Roman Catholics for the pursuit of agreed objectives does not imply acceptance of Roman Catholic doctrinal distinctives or endorsement of the Roman Catholic church system.

2. We understand the statement that "we are justified by grace through faith because of Christ" in terms of the substitutionary atonement and imputed righteousness of Christ, leading to full assurance of eternal salvation; we seek to testify in all circumstances and contexts to this, the historic Protestant understanding of salvation by faith alone (sola fide).

3. While we view all who profess to be Christian—Protestant and Catholic and Orthodox—with charity and hope, our confidence that anyone is truly a brother or sister in Christ depends not only on the content of his or her confession but on our perceiving signs of regeneration in his or her life.

4. Though we reject proselytizing as ECT defines it (that is "sheep stealing" for denominational aggrandizement), we hold that evangelism and church planting are always legitimate, whatever forms of church life are present already.

5. We think that the further theological discussions that ECT promised should begin as soon as possible.

> We make these applicatory clarifications of our commitment
> as supporters of ECT in order to prevent divisive
> misunderstandings of our beliefs and purposes.[32]

This document brought a sense of relief to some,[33] and understandably so, seeing that the signatories of the *Clarification* reaffirm a solid evangelical allegiance to salvation by faith *alone*. Yet when we probe further into the ECT/*Clarification* issue and see fully where those that signed the *Clarification* stand, we find a more entrenched inclusivism then what we would have ever dared expect.

First, as clear as the *Clarification* seems to be, one might expect the Catholic reaction to be antagonistic. However, this is not the case. To the contrary, "The Fort Lauderdale statement is to be warmly welcomed,"[34] says Richard Neuhaus. "Keith Fournier, a Catholic signer of the original document, remarked that though he did not think the Protestants' additional statement was necessary, it may reduce misunderstandings among evangelicals."[35] To the Catholics, this clarification did not threaten what was accomplished with the ECT document. In fact, even after their statement of clarification, they still maintained that ECT "is an invitation not to refight the wars of the past but to cross the threshold of hope into a Third Millennium of common witness and discipleship, including, please God, greater visible unity among all who follow Christ."[36]

I honestly wish that the Catholics were wrong in their perception of what was accomplished with ECT. But their perception was accurate, first in rightfully understanding the content of ECT, but also in appropriately understanding the content of the *Clarification*. For this latter document was never meant as a repudiation of ECT and the inclusivism that it promulgated. While written to repudiate supposed misunderstandings concerning the ECT document, the *Clarification* statement still defends ECT.

Even to Colson, the *Clarification* did not mean that he would deny Catholics a place within the Body of Christ. He explains himself in an article entitled "Why Catholics Are Our Allies":

> When confronting the non-Christian world—whether in
> evangelism or political activism—we should present a united
> front. This is the goal of ECT. The statement is candid
> about differences between the rooms; they are great and
> should not be trivialized. But its principal purpose is to

> gather Christians in the hallway, that arena of truth that
> unites all our traditions. . . . In becoming Christians, we all
> embrace a body of central truths, such as Creation, the Fall,
> substitutionary Atonement, and the infallibility of Scripture.
> But once inside the house, we find our fellowship within
> particular theological traditions.[37]

This is the paradox which presents evangelical inclusivism. No
matter how evangelical the ECT *Clarification* statement is, and no
matter how much it even stresses the need to uphold salvation by faith
alone, Colson can sign both it (the *Clarification*) and still hold to his
first premise (in ECT)—that Roman Catholicism still is within the
household of faith, no matter how wrong the Roman church might be
in some areas.

TOTAL PARADOX

J. I. Packer is another leader who personifies evangelical
inclusivism so well. As an original supporter of the ECT statement,
he has received many requests from concerned evangelicals to recant
his endorsement of its content.[38] But he says that before God he
cannot do otherwise than to stand with it. On the other hand, along
with Colson, he also has signed the *Clarification* statement.

Beyond that, he has also signed a statement entitled: "Resolutions
for Roman Catholic and Evangelical Dialogue" (known as the CURE
statement) which is strongly evangelical and seems to put in proper
perspective the Roman Catholic Church. For instance, it says, " . . .
we do not see this catholic consensus as a sufficient basis for
declaring that agreement exists on all the essential elements of the
Gospel."[39] It furthermore stresses that justification by faith alone is
"an essential of the Gospel on which radical disagreement continues,
and we deny the adequacy of any version of the Gospel that falls short
at this point."[40] Along with many other good statements, it also says:

> We deny, however, that in its present confession [the Roman
> Catholic Church] is an acceptable Christian communion, let
> alone being the mother of all the faithful to whom every
> believer needs to be related.[41]

However paradoxical it may seem, while Packer signed both the CURE statement and the *Clarification* statement of January 1995, he still sees no problem with the ECT document, nor does he see any problem with viewing orthodox Catholics (faithful to their own doctrine) as genuine brothers and sisters in Christ. He explains himself by saying:

> Do we recognize that good evangelical Protestants and good Roman Catholics—good, I mean, in terms of their own church's stated ideal of spiritual life—are Christians together? We ought to recognize this, for it is true.[42]

A little further down in the same article, he also included "good Eastern Orthodox" in his argument.[43] How can Packer, who knows the crucial differences between Catholicism and evangelicalism, defend "faith alone" and at the same time argue that Catholics and evangelicals are "Christians together"? This is evangelicalism inclusivism at its ultimate paradoxical level.

"THE GIFT OF SALVATION": FURTHERING ECT

October 7, 1997 saw the birth of another landmark in contemporary evangelicalism: the signing of a second joint statement by numerous evangelicals and Catholic leaders, this time called "The Gift of Salvation."[44] Timothy George, who took part in the adoption of this statement, explained that " 'The Gift of Salvation' directly addresses two important topics of perceived ambiguity in ECT: the doctrine of justification by faith alone and the biblical mandate for world missions and world evangelization."[45]

Concerning the first point of ambiguity, the 1994 ECT statement had made no clear mention that justification was by faith alone. On this point, R.C. Sproul sounded the alarm in his book, <u>Faith Alone</u>: "If *sola fide* [faith alone] is essential to the gospel and to Christianity and if Rome has not adopted *sola fide* as its doctrinal position, then *ECT* seriously betrays the gospel."[46]

The alarm was heard. However, it did not have much effect on the signers of ECT. In fact, it only heightened their paradoxical stance. In their joint statement, they have now included the belief in *sola fide* without making either the evangelicals or the Catholics change their previous understanding regarding justification.

While much in "The Gift of Salvation" is biblical, there is within it a few key statements which reveal that their basic thesis is flawed. This basic thesis is the same one advanced in ECT. It is that Catholics and evangelicals share a common bond of salvation in Jesus Christ. "The Gift of Salvation" states unequivocally:

> Through prayer and study of Holy Scripture, and aided by the Church's reflection on the sacred text from earliest times, we have found that, notwithstanding some persistent and serious differences, we can together bear witness to the gift of salvation in Jesus Christ.

> All who truly believe in Jesus Christ are brothers and sisters in the Lord and must not allow their differences, however important, to undermine this great truth, or to deflect them from bearing witness together to God's gift of salvation in Christ.[47]

This "witness together to God's gift of salvation" is said to be made on the basis of an agreement on the doctrine of justification by faith alone. In fact, it goes as far as to say, "We understand that what we here affirm is in agreement with what the Reformation traditions have meant by justification by faith alone *(soda fide)*."[48]

However, it also admits that the meaning of justification "has been much debated between Protestants and Catholics."[49] It acknowledges the difference as to "the historic uses of the language of justification as it relates to imputed and transformative righteousness."[50] Roman Catholicism has never repudiated its 16th century understanding of justification. If Catholics and evangelicals can agree to a term (justification by faith alone) but not to its exact definition, are they not playing with words when they say they "bear witness together"?

In fact, when all the acknowledged differences are considered, it is a wonder that the signers themselves even try to claim to bear "witness together to God's gift of salvation in Christ." The signers of "The Gift of Salvation" are not hesitant to reveal the content of their differences:

> While we rejoice in the unity we have discovered and are confident of the fundamental truths about the gift of salvation we have affirmed, we recognize that there are necessarily interrelated questions that require further and urgent exploration. Among such questions are these: the meaning of baptismal regeneration, the Eucharist, and sacramental grace; the historic uses of the language of justification as it relates to imputed and transformative righteousness; the normative status of justification in relation to all Christian doctrine; the assertion that while justification is by faith alone, the faith that receives salvation is never alone; diverse understandings of merit, reward, purgatory, and indulgences; Marian devotion and the assistance of the saints in the life of salvation; and the possibility of salvation for those who have not been evangelized.[51]

Most if not all of these differences have to do precisely with matters relating to salvation and how grace is obtained. Even a casual glance at the above paragraph reveals this: "baptismal *regeneration*," "sacramental grace," etc.

The most paradoxical statement comes in the conclusion of "The Gift of Salvation":

> As **Evangelicals** who thank God for *the heritage of the Reformation* and affirm with conviction its classic confessions, as **Catholics** who are *conscientiously faithful to the teaching of the Catholic Church*, and as **disciples together** of the Lord Jesus Christ who recognize our debt to our Christian forebears and our obligations to our contemporaries and those who will come after us, *we affirm our unity in the gospel* that we have here professed. In our continuing discussions, we seek no unity other than unity in the *truth*.[52]

How can evangelicals who profess the rightfulness of the Reformation claim to be disciples together with Catholics who are conscientiously faithful to the Catholic Church of old? It is this same Catholic

Church that the Reformers had condemned as a man-made religion. Also, it is this same Catholic Church that condemned the beliefs of the Reformers. Decidedly, the "truth" in which these people find unity has no more meaning.

ROMAN CATHOLICISM: WHAT ABOUT THE CHANGES?

The Catholic Church has long taught that it partakes of Christ's infallibility.[53] However, in light of Vatican II, it would be appropriate to ask, "Has the Roman Catholic Church changed since the 1960s?" Evangelicals and some fundamentalists might be seduced into thinking that the Catholic cooperation is evidence of a growing "evangelicalization" of the Catholic Church. However, though terminology is chosen more carefully, Catholic theology has not changed. The only major change since Vatican II is that they have essentially renounced their exclusive stance of centuries gone-by. This change now permits and encourages Catholic cooperation with inclusive evangelicals, since they no longer claim that evangelicals are anathema false teachers, but only "separated brethren."

The "exclusive" position of the Catholic Church was long entrenched in her body of doctrines. The Council of Florence (1442) declared:

> The Holy Roman Church firmly believes, confesses, and proclaims that outside the Catholic Church, no one, neither heathen nor Jew nor unbeliever nor schismatic, will have a share in eternal life, but will, rather, be subject to the everlasting fire which has been prepared for the Devil and his angels, unless he attaches himself to her (the Catholic Church) before his death.[54]

Much earlier Cyprian said, "He can no longer have God for his Father, who has not the Church for his mother."[55]

The Catholic Church also specified the lost nature of those who believed in salvation by faith alone. Consider the following canons of the Roman Catholic Church, which were made at the sixth session of the Council of Trent (16th century):

> If any one saith, that by faith alone the impious is justified; in such wise as to mean, that nothing else is required to co-operate

in order to the obtaining the grace of Justification, . . . let him be anathema (*Trent*, sess. 6. canon 9).

If any one saith, that justifying faith is nothing else but confidence in the divine mercy which remits sins for Christ's sake; or, that this confidence alone is that whereby we are justified; let him be anathema (*Trent*, sess. 6. canon 12).

If any one saith, that the justice received is not preserved and also increased before God through good works; but that the said works are merely the fruits and signs of Justification obtained, but not a cause of the increase thereof; let him be anathema (*Trent*, sess. 6. canon 24).

If any one saith, that the good works of one that is justified are in such manner the gifts of God, as that they are not also the good merits of him that is justified; or, that the said justified, by the good works which he performs through the grace of God and the merit of Jesus Christ, whose living member he is, does not truly merit increase of grace, eternal life, and the attainment of that eternal life,-if so be, however, that he depart in grace,-and also an increase of glory; let him be anathema (*Trent*, sess. 6. canon 32).[56]

According to those canons, those who hold to the evangelical faith are anathema.   But contrast those canons with the Roman Catholic declarations of Vatican II on ecumenism:

1) All who have been "justified by faith in baptism" are members of the Body of Christ; they all have the right to be called Christian; the children of the Catholic Church accept them as brothers.

2) The Catholic Church believes that the separated Churches and communities "are efficient in some respects." But the Holy Ghost makes use of these Churches; they are means of salvation to their members.

3) Catholics are encouraged to join in Oecumenical activity, and to meet non-Catholic Christians in truth and love. The task of "Oecumenical dialogue" belongs to theologians, competent authorities representing different Churches.

4) Catholics should not ignore their duty to other Christians—they should make the first approach. Even so, the primary duty of the Church at the present time is to discover what must be done within the catholic Church itself [sic]; to renew itself, to put its own house in order. Catholics sincerely believe that theirs is the Church of Christ; everything necessary must be done that others also may clearly recognize it as Christ's Church.
. . .

7) Between the Catholic Church and Western non-Catholic Christian communities, important differences remain; these differences are most evident in the interpretation of truth revealed by God. But the bonds of unity are already strong; their strength must be put to use. The bonds are, chiefly, the fact that Christians believe in the divinity of Christ and the fact of reverence for God's word revealed in the Bible.

8) In the cause of ecumenism, the Catholic must always remain true to the Faith that he has received. Impudent zeal in this matter is a hindrance to unity and not a help. So also is any attempt to achieve a merely superficial unity.[57]

That is why, according to Neuhaus, "ECT has generated very little controversy among Catholics."[58] He says:

Catholics are long accustomed to ecumenical initiatives, and have no difficulty in acknowledging that non-Catholic Christians are brothers and sisters in Christ who, by virtue of baptism and faith, are "truly but imperfectly in communion with the Catholic Church" (Vatican Council II).[59]

It is interesting to note that Catholics attribute our being Christian to baptism. To them, it is the sacrament of baptism that introduces a person into the Body of Christ. In *The Catechism of The Catholic Church*, it is written:

Holy Baptism is the basis of the whole Christian life, the gateway to life in the Spirit (vitae spiritualis ianua), and the door which gives access to the other sacraments. Through Baptism we are freed from sin and reborn as sons of God; we become members of Christ, are incorporated into the Church and made sharers in her mission: "Baptism is the sacrament of regeneration through water in the word."[60]

Thus, Catholics have changed their approach to those who teach a gospel contrary to theirs. Yet they have not renounced their theology of old, since they believe that, if evangelicals are brethren, it is because of baptism.[61] They do not really acknowledge that we have entered into Christianity by our "faith alone" conversion. According to the Catholics, if we have become Christian, it is in spite of our own beliefs. For baptism, to us evangelical Christians, is only a *symbol* of what happened to us when we believed and an *identification* with Christ as one of His followers. It is not what makes us a Christian. Yet, to the Catholic our baptism was enough to make us "truly but imperfectly in communion with the Catholic Church."[62]

Just as liberals had pled for "toleration" and unity, so also have the Catholics pled. This strategy of the Catholics has seen great fruit and the resulting inroads of Catholic acceptance in evangelical circles cannot be underestimated.

It is also important to note what Rome still teaches concerning Christ's work on the cross. The report on The Evangelical-Roman Catholic Dialogue on Mission (ERCDOM), says:

> Roman Catholics express Christ's death more in terms of 'solidarity.' In their understanding Jesus Christ in his death made a perfect offering of love and obedience to his Father, which recapitulated his whole life. In consequence, we can enter into the sacrifice of Christ and offer ourselves to the Father in and with him. For he became one with us in order that we might become one with him.[63]
>
> Vatican II defines the Church for Roman Catholics as 'the sacrament of salvation,' the sign and promise of redemption to each and every person without exception. . . . It is the mission of the Church to anticipate the Kingdom of God as liberation from the slavery of sin, from the slavery to the Law and from death; by the preaching of the gospel, by the forgiveness of sins and by the sharing in the Lord's Supper.[64]
>
> For Roman Catholics the gospel centres in the person, message and gracious activity of Christ. His life, death and resurrection are the foundation of the Church, and the Church carries the living gospel to the world. The Church is

> a real sacrament of the gospel. So the difference between us
> concerns the relationship between the gospel and the Church.
> In the one case, the gospel reconciles us to God through
> Christ and thus makes us a part of his people; in the other,
> the gospel is found within the life of his people, and thus we
> find reconciliation with God.[65]

The quotes could go on, for the twisting of God's grace into merit runs throughout their theology. I trust that enough has been said to reveal the heresy of the Roman Catholic Church, though it is "couched" now in better terms (see appendix A for more Roman Catholic doctrine).

"EVANGELICALLY COMMITTED ROMAN CATHOLICS"?

What about the so called "believing Catholics" or "evangelical Catholics"?[66] One would be inclined to wonder if the Catholics who have signed ECT might not fit that ambiguous label. After all, the *Clarification* statement claimed that their "para-church cooperation was with evangelically committed Roman Catholics." But upon examination, we find Neuhaus, and his Catholic co-signers, faithful to and representatives of, the Roman Catholic Church. Even the ECT document reveals this, since the acknowledged differences (as seen above) were not between Evangelicals and a supposed "evangelical" segment within Catholicism, but rather between the historical evangelical faith and orthodox Roman Catholicism.

Neuhaus himself, the Catholic leader of the ECT effort, is not "evangelically committed" in the historical sense of the term. He has commented on the issue of "faith alone":

> The *Catechism of the Catholic Church* does not reject the
> distinctive Reformation formula that justification is by grace
> alone through faith alone because of Christ alone. Neither
> does it affirm it. To address it at all would require going on
> to make clear that grace is not alone but confirms human
> freedom, that living faith is not alone but issues in a life of
> obedience, that Christ is not alone but always to be found in
> the company of His Church.[67]

Another example is Keith Fournier who also signed ECT. In fact, Fournier considers himself an evangelical Catholic Christian. He believes he can be evangelical by claiming to hold to the gospel and yet remain thoroughly Catholic. However, his thorough Catholicity colors his "evangelicity," so that he maintains the grace-giving efficiency of sacraments while rejecting not only a once-and-for-all type conversion—he's had several "conversions" himself—but also faith alone. His book is a classic example of how much modern Catholics can sound pious but still be in darkness by rejecting God's simple plan of salvation.[68]

THE UNDERLYING FACTORS OF CURRENT EVANGELICAL INCLUSIVISM

When one understands the major differences between Catholics and evangelicals, how can one claim the biblical gospel and still consider the Catholic Church a "sister denomination"? This question is basic in importance. In the following pages, the outlines of the answer will take shape.

1. *The Gospel, as Evangelically Defined, Is Only a View*

Consider what Timothy George, senior editor of *Christianity Today*, has said concerning ECT.

> Here is an ecumenism of the trenches born out of a common moral struggle to proclaim and embody the gospel of Jesus Christ to a culture in disarray. . . . However, lest anyone be carried away by the ecumenical euphoria of the moment, it needs to be stated clearly that the Reformation was not a mistake. . . . *Both the formal and material principles of the Reformation—that is, the infallibility of Holy Scripture and justification by faith—are duly affirmed in this statement* [ECT]. But how these principles relate to a host of other issues such as church authority, sacramental efficacy, and authentic ministry are acknowledged points of difference.[69]

Evangelicals that claim belief in the biblical gospel can consider Roman Catholicism part of authentic Christianity because they make out the doctrines of salvation and grace as being mere *views*, rather than exclusive truths from God's Word. *As long as Catholics can sign to "justification by faith in Christ," they can be considered brothers and sisters in Christ, no matter how they define it.*

Ralph Covell, in his article, "The Christian Gospel and World Religions: How much Have American Evangelicals Changed?" presents Roman Catholics as believing the gospel, but in a different way. He says, "The basic point of disagreement was over the extent of salvation and the way it is mediated."[70] Does not the Bible define the way salvation is mediated? Or is this just a matter of one's thoughts? Inclusivists suggest the latter.

The ERCDOM report, edited by Stott and Meeking, says:

> Although many Evangelicals will admit that their presentation of the gospel is often one-sided or defective, yet they could not contemplate any evangelism in which the good news of God's justification of sinners by his grace in Christ through faith alone is not proclaimed. . . . [Roman Catholics] would not necessarily want to deny the validity of the message which Evangelicals preach, but would say that important aspects of the gospel are missing from it. . . . *So long as each side regards the other's view of the gospel as defective, there exists a formidable obstacle to be overcome.* This causes us a particular sorrow in our dialogue on mission, in which we have come to appreciate one another and to discover unexpected agreements. . . .[71]

Notice the term "defective." Each side regards the other's view of the gospel as only *defective*. Stott and the evangelicals with him do not argue for the full *illegitimacy* of the Catholic gospel. That is why the report can read:

> We do not think that either Evangelicals or Roman Catholics should hesitate to join in common prayer when they meet in each other's homes. . . . In the name of Christ, Roman Catholics and Evangelicals can serve human need together. . . . We have neither ignored, nor discounted, nor even minimized them [the elements that divide]. For they are real, and in some cases serious. . . . *At the same time, we know and have experienced that the walls of our separation do not reach to heaven.* There is much that unites us, and

much in each other's different manifestations of Christian faith and life which we have come to appreciate. . . . Although faith may still in part separate us, love for the neighbour should unite us. . . . We believe that the most fruitful kind of Evangelical-Roman Catholic dialogue arises out of joint Bible study. For, as this report makes clear, both sides regard the Bible as God's Word, and acknowledge the need to read, study, believe and obey it. It is surely through the Word of God that, illumined by the Spirit of God, we shall progress toward greater agreement. . . . Honest and charitable dialogue is beneficial to those who take part in it; it enriches our faith, deepens our understanding, and fortifies and clarifies our convictions. It is also a witness in itself, inasmuch as it testifies to the desire for reconciliation and meanwhile expresses a love which encompasses even those who disagree.[72]

In his article on the issue, Alister McGrath argues first that "although some evangelicals continue to insist that the Roman Catholic church officially teaches justification by works, this is not true."[73]   Then, ironically, he claims to be aware of, and does acknowledge, Catholic belief in indulgences, purgatory, the seven sacraments, and other issues such as canon of Scripture, sufficiency of Scripture, and the role of Mary.[74]   He also complains about one point in the new *Catechism of the Catholic Church*:

While emphasizing that salvation takes place by grace, on the basis of the work of Christ rather than on human effort or achievement, the catechism seems reluctant to engage with the questions raised above [on the Reformation] and does little to reassure the anxieties of any readers familiar with the sixteenth-century debates. It is clear that the agenda of the Reformation remains with us on these issues. . . .[75]

He then goes on to say:

The catechism's robust and committed defense of orthodoxy will be a major consideration for evangelicals as they reconsider their attitude to Roman Catholicism. It indicates that an important ally could be at hand in the struggle for the restoration of doctrinal orthodoxy to the mainline denominations.[76]

He suggests that there are two options for evangelicals in dealing with Catholicism: 1) refuse to have anything to do with Roman Catholics, or 2) collaborate with Roman Catholics on a limited range of issues, while acknowledging that differences still remain on others.

Regarding the first option, he states, "Can feuds between Christians be allowed when non-Christians seem to be winning the cultural battles? A divided Christianity is simply a weakened Christianity."[77] Since his premise is that, in spite of some differences Catholics and evangelicals are both genuine Christians, he recommends the second option. His basis is this: "Here we also find a mutual defense of Christian orthodoxy against liberalism, secularism, and non-Christian religions."[78] Therefore, no matter how serious he might claim the differences between evangelicals and Catholics to be, these differences are not essential enough to the gospel to prevent one from considering Catholicism as a genuine and orthodox expression of the Body of Christ.

J. I. Packer is another clear example of someone who considers doctrines on salvation as mere views:

> May ECT realistically claim, as in effect it does, that its evangelical and Catholic drafters agree on the gospel of salvation? Yes and no. If you mean, could they all be relied on to attach the same small print to their statement, "we are justified by grace through faith because of Christ," no. (The Tridentine assertion of merit and the Reformational assertion of imputed righteousness can hardly be harmonized.) If you mean, do all present-day Catholics focus on the living Christ, Lord, Savior, and coming King as the direct object of the sinner's faith and hope in the way ECT does, doubtless no again. (I imagine some traditional Catholics have problems with ECT at this point, though today's Catholic theologians observably do not.) But if you mean, does ECT's insistence that the Christ of Scripture, creeds, and confessions is faith's proper focus, and that "Christian witness is of necessity aimed at conversion," not only as an initial step but as a personal life-process, and that *this constitutes a sufficient account of the gospel of salvation* for shared evangelistic ministry, then surely yes. What brings salvation, after all, is not *any theory* about faith in Christ, justification, and the church, but faith itself in Christ himself.[79]

The above statement is very explicit and full of implications. Packer reveals that his acceptance of Catholicism is not due to ignorance or misunderstanding of Catholic doctrine. It is instead due to considering the biblical content of the gospel, *not as self-authoritative and objective in its meaning,* but rather *as open to various human explanations and views.*

2. *Redefinition of Essential Christianity/Redefinition of the Gospel*

Packer's phrase "*this constitutes a sufficient account of the gospel of salvation* for shared evangelistic ministry" gives a second element of the answer to the basic question: "How can one both claim the biblical gospel and still consider the Catholic Church a sister 'denomination'?" Removing the issues of "theories about faith in Christ, justification, and the church," he reduces the requirement for salvation to merely "faith itself in Christ himself" without biblically defining this faith. The *simplification*—read *redefinition*—of the gospel is the second aspect that permits an evangelical to consider Catholicism to be a legitimate expression of Christianity.

An article in *Christianity Today* states:

> The document [ECT] acknowledges "deep and longstanding theological differences between evangelicals and Catholics." Either stated or implied throughout, however, is the assertion that these differences do not have *an impact on Christianity's core of essential beliefs* and thus should not prevent the communities from working together.[80]

In his book, The Body, Colson sets out to define Christianity's core of essential beliefs:

> • God the creator exists in three persons, Father, Son and Holy Spirit.
> • Born of the virgin, He suffered, died, rose again, and was exalted at the right hand of the Father from whence He will come again.
> • The Holy Spirit brings the benefits of Christ's saving work to people who believe in Him.
> • Christians are expected to unite with a local church, submit to the authority of bishops and elders, live a holy life conducive to the spread of the gospel.

• God will judge the world and receive His own at the end of history.[81]

The key then, according to the evangelical inclusivists, is to reduce the gospel to a minimal and undefined set of core beliefs. Thus, the issues of dissension on justification, regeneration and saving faith are eliminated from the core, permitting evangelicals to claim spiritual fellowship with the Catholics.

MAIN-LINE EVANGELICAL INCLUSIVISM

Evangelical inclusivism is not necessarily embraced by some radicals who espouse the term "evangelical" against its historical meaning. As we have seen, the alarming truth is that some evangelicals who would argue strongly for the historical evangelical faith—even for faith alone—still consider as genuine Christians those whose faith in God is anything but evangelical. Consequently, some who claim to believe in the biblical gospel fully endorse false gospels. The problem that confronts these evangelical inclusivists is, therefore, not necessarily their personal *view* of the gospel but rather their *approach* to the gospel. This approach denies any biblical objectivity in regards to the content of the gospel.

Is this inclusivism regarding the gospel widespread in evangelicalism, or is it isolated? Though there are still many evangelicals who reject embracing Catholicism as part of the family of God at large, this inclusive element should not be underestimated. For instance, McGrath has said:

> The consensus that appears to be emerging among younger evangelicals corresponds broadly to the second approach outlined above [consider Catholics as brothers while acknowledging the differences (quoted earlier on p. 92)]. This general outlook suggests that in a world with both dangers and opportunities for the Christian gospel, at least in the short term, there is a real need for Christians to set their differences aside and support and defend their common ideas and values. When the world is a safer place for the gospel, we can get back to sorting out some of the issues that have

temporarily been set aside in this way. And we might even learn something from each other along the way.[82]

McGrath himself, though uneasy with the pragmatism of what he suggests, concedes "that it may hold the key to some very needed reconciliation and cooperation in the body of Christ."[83]

PROMISE KEEPERS — A SIGN OF THE TIMES

Such ecumenical and inclusive cooperation is already taking place in many sectors of evangelicalism. The recent birth and surge in popularity of the Promise Keepers movement would suggest this. Promise Keepers (PK) includes in its very core covenant the promise of taking down denominational barriers.[84] Catholics, Baptists, Pentecostals, and others within Christendom are welcome.[85] Love for Jesus is what counts, but to define biblically what that love consists of is unwelcome since that would not tear down, but rather build up or maintain the walls of division.

It is important to remember that since the downfall of orthodoxy earlier this century many in the main Protestant denominations no longer preach the biblical gospel. Liberalism is rampant in the mainline Protestant denominations. Mix in many evangelicals with those denominations and add to that the sacramental denominations such as Catholicism and the Church of England, and you have a religious melting pot of people gathered in Christ's name, without any definite statement of faith regarding the gospel. The numerous stadiums across North America filled with enthusiastic PK attenders attest to the success PK has had in breaking down barriers and in promoting inclusivism.

However, what is happening in the Promise Keepers movement is only a reflection of the trend taking place on a larger scale within evangelicalism. On this trend, Packer says:

> Billy Graham's cooperative evangelism, in which all the churches in an area, of whatever stripe, are invited to share, is well established on today's Christian scene. And so are charismatic get togethers . . . where the distinction between Protestant and Catholic vanishes in a Christ-centered unity of experience. So the togetherness that ECT pleads for has

already begun. ECT, then, must be viewed as fuel for a fire that is already alight. The grassroots coalition at which the document aims is already growing. . . . ECT is playing catch-up to the Holy Spirit, formulating at the level of principle a commitment into which many have already entered at the level of practice. . . .[86]

CONCLUSION

The 20th century has seen many developments in Christendom. Perhaps the most significant and, paradoxically, the most ignored development has been the growth of a subtle and deadly inclusivism within the community of those who claim the biblical gospel. This inclusivism is responsible for the ultimate downfall of orthodoxy within the mainline denominations. It is also responsible for building a bridge between the evangelical community and the Roman Catholic Church. It legitimizes false gospels and it gives hope to those who have none.

This inclusive element within evangelicalism may come with various slants. It may make room for those who have never heard, for the pious liberal, or for the orthodox Catholic, but in the end, this inclusivism within evangelical ranks is nothing less than a subtle yet definite departure from the gospel of Jesus Christ. The gospel is reduced and redefined to a very generic core set of beliefs. The authoritative, objective and exclusive teachings of the Scripture concerning the gospel are "relativized" as only matters of opinion. Perhaps Colson, quoting Neuhaus, best defines *inclusivism* in this context. He says:

> . . . one should engage in "the most vigorous advocacy of what one believes to be right," but at the same time make "a mutual pledge of allegiance to reverence one with another within the mystery of our being a people led by God toward that time in which we shall 'know even as we are known.' "[87]

The inclusivism which is promoted more and more within evangelicalism must be recognized, exposed and shunned as an enemy to the gospel. Rather than promoting an inclusive acceptance of false gospels, Paul said: "But though we, or an angel from heaven, preach any other gospel unto you than that which we have preached unto you, let him be accursed" (Gal. 1:8). The true gospel makes no room for false gospels, and neither will anyone who fully embraces the true gospel of Jesus Christ.

> *[Inclusivism is] the paradox of asserting both ultimate commitment to one's own religion and total openness to another's religion.*
> — David Bosh, advocating inclusivism[88]

NOTES ON CHAPTER 3

1. Packer, "Crosscurrents among Evangelicals," 172-173. He went on to say: "Might it be as responding to the Holy Spirit, formulating at the level of principle a commitment into which there has already been entry at the level of practice? It seems clear that the burden of proof must rest on any who wish to deny that this is so. . . . ECT is a good beginning. I stand with it (I cannot do otherwise) and for it I thank God. Now I wait to see what God will do with it."

2. Wilson Ewin, "Congress 85: Tragedy in New England," *Baptist Bulletin* (May 1985): 11-12, 33.

3. This is the usual context of the term "inclusivism" in current theological literature.

4. B. Meeking and J. Stott, eds., The Evangelical-Roman Catholic Dialogue on Mission, 1977-1984. A Report (Exeter: Paternoster, 1986), 46.

5. "The salvation of the Gentiles— Implication for Other Faiths," *Evangelical Review of Theology* (January 1991): 36-43; Evert D. Osburn, "Those who Have Never Heard: Have they No Hope," *Evangelical Review of Theology* (January 1991): 44-50; Evert D. Osburn, "Those who have never heard, Have They Hope?" *Jets* (September 1989): 367-372; Colin Chapman, "Going Soft on Islam," *Vox Evangelica* (1989): 7-31; M. Erickson, "Hope for Those Who Have Never Heard? Yes, But..." *Evangelical Missions Quarterly* (April 1975):

122-125; Clark H. Pinnock, <u>A Wideness in God's Mercy</u> (Grand Rapids: Zondervan Publishing House, 1992); John Saunders, <u>No Other Name</u> (Grand Rapids: William B. Eerdmans Publishing Company, 1992). See also William V. Crockett and James G. Sigountos, eds., <u>Through No Fault of their Own?</u> (Grand Rapids: Baker Book House, 1991). Ramesh P. Richard makes a good rebuttal of the inclusive view in his article, "Soteriological Inclusivism and Dispensationalism," *Bibliotheca Sacra* (January-March 1994): 85-108.

6. Bruce Nicholls, "The Salvation and Lostness of Mankind," *Evangelical Review of Theology* (January 1991): 19.

7. Ibid., 20.

8. Ibid.

9. M. Erickson, "Hope for Those Who Have Never Heard? Yes, But..." *Evangelical Missions Quarterly* (April 1975): 124-125.

10. For a detailed and Biblical rebuttal to this kind of inclusivism, see Ramesh P. Richard, "Soteriological Inclusivism and Dispensationalism," *Bibliotheca Sacra* (January-March 1994): 85-108. See also his book, <u>The Population of Heaven - A Biblical Response to the inclusivist position on who will be saved</u> (Chicago: Moody Press, 1994).

11. James Davison Hunter, <u>Evangelicalism: The Coming Generation</u> (Chicago: The University of Chicago Press, 1987), 37.

12. Ibid.,162-163, emphasis added; see also Erickson's article, "The Fate of Those Who Never Hear," *Bibliotheca Sacra* (January-March 1995): 3-15. He says:
    However, in recent years controversy has arisen about these concepts. The uniqueness, exclusiveness, and necessity of Jesus Christ and belief in Him for salvation are being questioned. . . . First, it is important to address this subject because confusion has arisen regarding salvation and Christ, even in circles where this has traditionally been given the highest value. The Barna organization's polling data published in 1992 indicated a rather high degree of correct understanding of the basis of salvation. When asked to describe their belief about life after death, 62 percent of the respondents agreed that "When you die, you will go to heaven because you have confessed your sins and have accepted Jesus Christ as your savior." Only six percent said people go to heaven "because God loves all people and will not let them perish." However, when asked to respond to the statement, "All good people, whether they consider Jesus Christ to be their Savior or not, will live in heaven after they die on earth," those who disagreed outnumbered those who agreed by less than a five to four ratio! Probably this means that the emotional factor has overwhelmed the rational. . . .
    A change in evangelicalism may also be hinted at in other statements, such as one from Nicholls: "The advocacy of universalism goes back to Origen, but until recent time has been a minority view. Today it is a live option for both Protestant and Catholic scholars" [Nicholls, "The Salvation and Lostness of Mankind," 18].

13. See Carl F. H. Henry, "The Ecumenical Age: Problems and Promise," *Bibliotheca Sacra* (July 1966): 204-219.

14. Chuck Colson, The Body (Dallas: Word Publishing, 1992), 87.

15. Ibid., 88.

16. Ibid., 106.

17. Illustrative of the backing Colson has received in the writing of his book are the following citations found on the back cover of his book, The Body:

"With punchy prose and haunting stories, Colson challenges, humbles, and inspires. If you are willing to be made uncomfortable in the cause of real and deep church renewal, this is the book for you. It comes from the heart; may it go to the heart." —J.I. PACKER, professor of theology, Regent College

"Although as a Catholic I would find it imperative to add some clarifications to the authors' notion of Church, The Body is a deep moving and significant work. An eloquent reminder of what unites us in the Lord as we struggle to make His word heard." —JOHN CARDINAL O'CONNOR, Archbishop of New York

"Absolute required reading for anyone who considers himself or herself a part of the world-wide body of Christ." —PAT ROBERTSON, founder, Christian Broadcasting Network

" . . . why is it that every time I read a Colson book I sincerely resolve, before God, to become a riskier Christian. Readers, beware!" —BILL HYBELS, senior pastor, Willow Creek Community Church

"There is enough here to offend almost everyone. After you are offended you will be convicted, and after you are convicted, you will be changed." —STEVE BROWN, president, Key Life Network, Inc.

"Chuck Colson is clearly 'God's Statesman' who, in The Body, puts . . . all the saints in true perspective—all part of his church. His best book." —DR. JERRY FALWELL, chancellor, Liberty University

"It attacks many false ideas of the church. I was convicted, stirred, challenged, and encouraged as I read it." —DR. JAMES M. BOICE, minister, Tenth Presbyterian Church, Philadelphia

" . . . a tremendous blend of the practical as well as the perceptive. The sensitivity with which we are all called together—as diverse members but united under Jesus' Lordship—is a confirming 'word.' No thoughtful Christian can deny this call." —JACK HAYFORD, pastor, The Church on the Way

"A pace-setting volume that stretches beyond Geneva, Rome, and Wheaton in quest of an adequate doctrine of the church." —DR. CARL F. H. HENRY, lecturer and author

" . . . provocative, compelling, and pertinent. All may not agree with every word, but all who care about the church should carefully read The Body." —ADRIAN ROGERS, pastor, Bellevue Baptist Church

"In some ways The Body is Chuck Colson's finest book. All who read it will be enlightened." —KENNETH S. KANTZER, senior editor, *Christianity Today*

"Christians of all communions will be richly rewarded by this lively reflection on the inescapable unity of Christ and the church." —RICHARD JOHN NEUHAUS, editor-in-chief, *First Things*

"A blunt, hard-hitting diagnosis of what's wrong with the church. It stands in the tradition of the prophetic classics." —VERNON GROUNDS, professor, Denver Seminary

18. The WCC is not evangelical and is liberal in many ways. See Tormod Engelsviken, "Ecumenical or evangelical—is there any difference," *Themelios* (Jan/Feb. 1991): 10-13, which discusses the differences between the WCC and the LCWE (which is evangelical).

19. John Stapert, "An Ecumenical Spring," *Perspectives* (April 1991): 3, emphasis added.

20. Tony Lane, "Evangelicalism and Roman Catholicism," *Evangelical Quarterly* (October 1989): 363.

21. Ibid.

22. See first foot note of the Introduction.

23. "Evangelical-Catholic pact questioned," *Christian Century* (March 15, 1995): 287.

24. Randy Frame, "Evangelicals, Catholics Pursue New Cooperation," *Christianity Today* (May 16, 1994): 53.

25. "Evangelicals & Catholics Together: The Christian Mission in the Third Millennium," *First Things* (May 1994): 15-22.

26. Ibid.

27. Ibid, emphasis added.

28. As quoted by Randy Frame, in "Evangelicals, Catholics Pursue New Cooperation," *Christianity Today* (May 16, 1994): 53.

29. E.g., John F. MacArthur, <u>Reckless Faith</u> (Wheaton, IL: Crossway Books, 1994).

30. E.g., Timothy George (senior editor), "Catholics and Evangelicals in the Trenches," *Christianity Today* (May 16, 1994): 16-17.

31. E.g., Gary Corwin, "House United or Unequal Yoke?" *Evangelical Quarterly Missions* (July 1995): 276-277; Augustin B. Vencer Jr., "An International Perspective on Evangelical-Catholic Cooperation," *Evangelical Missions Quarterly* (July 1995): 278-279; Kenneth S. Kantzer, "Should Roman Catholics and Evangelicals Join Ranks?" *Christianity Today* (July 18, 1994): 17.

32. Richard John Neuhaus, "Nobody Said it Would Be Easy," *First Things* (May 1995): 78-79.

33. Gary Corwin, "House United or Unequal Yoke?" *Evangelical Missions Quarterly* (July 1995): 276-277.

34. Neuhaus, "Nobody Said It Would Be Easy," 78-79.

35. "Evangelical-Catholic pact questioned," *Christian Century* (March 15, 1995): 287-288.

36. Neuhaus, "Protestant Reformation and Universal Church," *First Things* (March 1995): 70.

37. Charles Colson, "Why Catholics Are Our Allies," *Christianity Today*

(November 14, 1994): 136.

38. J. I. Packer, "Crosscurrents among Evangelicals," in Evangelicals & Catholics Together: Toward a Common Mission, eds. Charles Colson and Richard John Neuhaus (Dallas: Word Publishing, 1995), 148.

39. Evangelicals & Catholics Together: Toward a Common Mission, eds. Charles Colson and Richard John Neuhaus (Dallas: Word Publishing, 1995), 157-159.

40. Ibid.

41. Ibid.

42. J. I. Packer, "Why I Signed It," *Christianity Today* (December 12,1994): 35.

43. Ibid.

44. Timothy George, ed., "The Gift of Salvation," *Christianity Today* (December 8, 1997): 34f. The document is reproduced in full in Appendix B.

45. Timothy George, "Evangelicals and Catholics Together: A New Initiative," *Christianity Today* (December 8, 1997): 34f.

46. R.C. Sproul, Faith Alone (Grand Rapids: Baker Books, 1995), 43, emphasis original.

47. "The Gift of Salvation," 34f.

48. Ibid.

49. Ibid.

50. Ibid.

51. Ibid.

52. Ibid, emphasis added.

53. For instance, consider the paragraphs 889 and 890 of the *Catechism of the Catholic Church*:

> 889 In order to preserve the Church in the purity of the faith handed on by the apostles, Christ who is the Truth willed to confer on her a share in his own infallibility. By a "supernatural sense of faith" the People of God, under the guidance of the Church's living Magisterium, "unfailingly adheres to this faith."
>
> 890 The mission of the Magisterium is linked to the definitive nature of the covenant established by God with his people in Christ. It is this Magisterium's task to preserve God's people from deviations and defections and to guarantee them the objective possibility of professing the true faith without error. Thus, the pastoral duty of the Magisterium is aimed at seeing to it that the People of God abides in the truth that liberates. To fulfill this service, Christ endowed the Church's shepherds with the charism of infallibility in matters of faith and morals. . . .
>
> Quoted from URL: <http://www.christusrex.org/www1/CDHN/church4.html> (current version 18 Jan 1999).

54. David J. Bosh, "The Church in Dialogue: From Self-Delusion to Vulnerability," *Missiology: An International Review* (16:2, April 1988): 135.

55. The Ante-Nicene Fathers, Vol. V, 423.

56. Quoted from the World Wide Web, at URL:
    <http://history.hanover.edu/early/trent/ct06jc.htm>
    (current version 27 Jan 1999).

57. Vatican II, The Decree On Ecumenism. Quoted from URL:
    <http://www.christusrex.org/www1/CDHN/v1.html>
    (current version 9 Sept 1997).

58. Richard John Neuhaus, "A Sense of Change Both Ominous and Promising," *First Things* (August/September 1995): 67-68.

59. Ibid.

60. *The Catechism of The Catholic Church*, para. 1213. Quoted from the World Wide Web, at URL:<http://www.christusrex.org/www1/CDHN/ccc_cont.html> (current version 6 Oct 1997).

61. Keith Fournier, Catholic signer of ECT, puts it this way, " . . . *all those justified by faith through baptism* are incorporated into Christ. They therefore have a right to be honored by the title Christian, and are properly regarded as brothers in the Lord by the Sons of the Catholic Church" [Fournier, Evangelical Catholics, 16, emphasis added].

62. Vatican II, The Decree On Ecumenism. Quoted from URL:
    <http://www.christusrex.org/www1/CDHN/v1.html>
    (current version 9 Sept 1997).

63. Meeking and Stott, 39.

64. Ibid., 30.

65. Ibid., 44-45.

66. E.g., Kantzer, "Pastoral Letters and the Realities of Life" *Christianity Today* (March 1, 1985): 12. If any Catholic is a genuine believer, he does so against the grain of the Roman Catholic Church. The terms "believing Catholic" or "evangelical Catholic" are misnomers; they create ambiguity. If used, one should clarify what he means. The case of Keith Fournier, who considers himself an evangelical Catholic, might be useful to caution Evangelicals from potential naivety. Whatever "evangelical moments"—as he calls them—he might have had, he still holds to all the orthodox teachings of Roman Catholicism [Fournier, Evangelical Catholics, 17].

67. Neuhaus, "Protestant Reformation and Universal Church," *First Things* (March 1995): 70. It is hard to see how any logic is preserved in Neuhaus' statement.

How can he say "faith alone . . . is not rejected," then say: "grace is not alone . . . living faith is not alone . . . Christ is not alone . . ."?

68. See Fournier's book: <u>Evangelical Catholics</u> (Nashville: Thomas Nelson Publishers, 1990).

69. Timothy George (senior editor), "Catholics and Evangelicals in the Trenches," *Christianity Today* (May 16, 1994): 16, emphasis added.

70. Ralph R. Covell, "The Christian Gospel and World Religions: How much Have American Evangelicals Changed?" *IBMR* (January 1991): 14.

71. Meeking and Stott, 81-86 *passim*, emphasis added.

72. Meeking and Stott, 89, emphasis added.

73. Alister McGrath, "Do We Still Need the Reformation?" *Christianity Today* (December 12, 1994): 30; see also p. 29.

74. Ibid., 31-32.

75. Ibid., 31.

76. Ibid., 29.

77. Ibid., 33.

78. Ibid.

79. J. I. Packer, "Why I Signed It," *Christianity Today* (December 12, 1994): 37, emphasis added. In a similar statement in his article "Crosscurrents among Evangelicals" in <u>Evangelicals & Catholics Together: Toward a Common Mission</u>, Packer said:

> Certainly, the Tridentine assertion of merit and the Reformational assertion of imputed righteousness can hardly be harmonized, and no doubt there are many Catholics today, as there are certainly many Protestants, who do not focus on the living Christ as Lord, Savior, and coming King, or make him the direct object of their faith and hope. (I imagine some traditional Catholics, for whom the Church rather than Christ is the primary focus of faith, will have problems with ECT at this point, though today's Catholic theologians observably do not.) But surely ECT's insistence that the Christ of Scripture and the creeds is faith's proper object, and that "Christian witness is of necessity aimed at conversion," both as an initial step and also as a personal life-process, constitutes a sufficient account of the gospel for shared evangelistic ministry. Evangelism seeks to lead people into salvation, and what brings them salvation is not any theory about faith and justification, but trusting Jesus himself as Lord, Master, and divine Savior . . . " [p. 168].

80. Randy Frame, "Evangelicals, Catholics Pursue New Cooperation," *Christianity Today* (May 16, 1994): 53, emphasis added.

81. Colson, <u>The Body</u>, 108, 109.

82. McGrath, 33.

83. Ibid.

84. Janssen, Al and Larry K. Weeken, eds., <u>Seven Promises of a Promise Keeper</u> (Colorado Springs, CO: Focus on the Family Publishing, 1994), 169ff.

85. Pickering reports:
> Randy Phillips, president of Promise Keepers was asked: "On the issue of Catholicism, does Promise Keepers have a policy on how to interact with Roman Catholics?" Phillips responded: "What we do care about is do you love Jesus and are you born again by the Spirit of God? And so if you have been born again by the Spirit of God, then whatever the labels are should not divide us. So from that standpoint all men are welcome . . . whether you're Baptist, Pentecostal, or Roman Catholic. If you are in the Body of Christ, then you should certainly be welcome."
>
> The founder of Promise Keepers, Bill McCartney, echoed the same: "Promise Keepers doesn't care if you're Pentecostal. Do you love Jesus? . . . Hear me. Promise Keepers doesn't care if you're Catholic. Do you love Jesus?" [sic][Ernest D. Pickering, <u>Promise Keepers and the Forgotten Promise</u>, pamphlet (Decatur, AL: Baptist World Mission, n.d.), 9].

86. Packer, "Why I Signed It," 36.

87. Colson, <u>The Body</u>, 107.

88. "The Church in Dialogue: From Self-Delusion to Vulnerability," *Missiology* (April 1988): 143.

Part 2

COUNTERING
INCLUSIVISM

When the apostles faced false doctrine, their response was to proclaim and reaffirm the truth. For example, Paul's letter to the Galatians reaffirms salvation by grace alone, through faith alone, and John's first epistle reaffirms belief in the deity and the humanity of the Son of God. In countering evangelical inclusivism, it is necessary to define the biblically revealed essentials of the faith.

But before we do that in our last chapter, it will be important to go to the root of the problem of inclusivism which is its concept of revealed truth. What does the Scripture say of itself? How are we to approach the concept of truth? We will attempt to give answers to questions such as these in the coming chapter.

Chapter 4

A BIBLICAL APPROACH
TO TRUTH

The Bible repeatedly reminds us of its own clarity, its own ability to be understood rightly, not only by scholars or specialists, but by all believers. . . . Not once do we hear Jesus saying anything like the following: "I see how your problem arose—the Scriptures are not very clear on that subject." Instead, whether he is speaking to scholars or to untrained common people, his responses always assume that the blame for misunderstanding any teaching of Scripture is not to be placed on the Scriptures themselves but on those who misunderstand or fail to accept what is written.
— Wayne A. Grudem[1]

T HE DAY IS BUT BEGINNING, yet the atmosphere is tense. A man is deeply troubled, grasping for fleeting solutions. He questions, he turns, he probes. But the forthcoming answers are not those he expected. Finally, he concludes the discussion. His voice, cold with disbelief and skepticism, rings out with finality, "What is truth?!" Then he turns away. . . .

Two thousand years later, Pilate's question to Jesus is still echoing in the hearts and minds of many, with such questions as:

"How can we know?"
"Who should we believe?"
"Why would I be wrong and not you?"
"Isn't that just your opinion?"
"How do you know you're right?"

All these questions are perfectly summed up in Pilate's question: "What is truth?"

The answer to which the vast majority of people are turning is the same one implied by Pilate's question: there is no ultimate truth, only a vast amalgam of "truths." There is but one absolute according to the modern secular man, and that is that *there are no absolutes.* Everything is relative (except, of course, the statement "everything is relative").

The lure of relativism is only amplified by the fact that we are six billion people living on this earth, and all of us have one opinion (at least). That makes for quite a diversity of opinions, and the means to communicate them is not lacking in efficiency. With this plethora of opinions, what is more socially acceptable than to claim that everyone is right in his own way?

In fact, even some evangelical theologians and authors are now arguing for this "up-to-date" view of truth. Philip D. Kenneson could not put it more plainly in the title of his chapter: "There's No Such Thing as Objective Truth, and It's a Good Thing, Too."[2] Authors J. Richard Middleton and Brian J. Walsh of Toronto's Institute for Christian Study write along the same line:

> Since all worldviews in a postmodern reading are merely inventions, decisively conditioned by the social context in which they occur, and certainly not given to us by either nature or revelation, any "truth" we claim for our cherished positions must be kept strictly in quotation marks.[3]

If we follow this line of thinking, how nicely will we fit into the social climate of the day. We will be able to claim the "truth" yet contradict no one.

This situation reminds me of an anecdote. While in seminary, I had a friend, a fellow student, with whom I often studied for exams. Of course, when we quizzed each other, our answers were not always right. So often I had to hear, "Sorry, the answer is. . . ." I devised a way to save face (jokingly, of course) in those embarrassing situations. When I was corrected, I would simply say off-handedly, "Yea, that's true <u>too</u>." In this way, I could recognize that he was right without admitting that I was wrong.

THAT'S TRUE TOO! — THE MOTTO OF OUR AGE

Such an expression, though used in jest, is quite representative of today's thinking. No one has to be wrong. Everyone can be right. "You don't see it as I do? No problem. There is room for both of us to be right, each in his own way." As Gary Phillips puts it: "One may venture to say, 'This is true,' so long as one does not add, 'therefore that is false.' "[4]

What is the nature of truth?[5] Is it absolute and objective, or is it subjective and relative? The answers to these questions are far more obvious than some would argue. For instance, can two contradictory opinions both be true? Can the one who thinks tomorrow is Friday be as correct as the one who thinks tomorrow is Thursday? Of course not. What if the one who is wrong is sincere? What if he had good intentions? Is he still wrong? Yes, of course. No one would argue with such evident facts. As one author puts it:

> To function in daily life, one must assume that truth is absolute (apparently the "truth" of an oncoming train motivates speculative relativists and absolutists alike to move out of the way).[6]

Yet for matters that are not as immediately verifiable, people often revert to their "that's true too!" motto.[7] That is why spiritual matters or religious issues are almost automatically relegated to the sphere of relativity. Why? Because spiritual matters are not as verifiable as, for instance, the days of the week. In fact, the truth regarding man and his destiny will be clearly evidenced only after this present life.

Reality in spiritual matters can never be proven during our fallen human existence.

Has not God told us that we walk by faith, not by sight (2 Cor. 5:7)? Of course we are not able to absolutely *prove* to ourselves or to others the truthfulness of our Christian claims. But our inability to "prove" our message to a lost world should not alarm us, since we can only "walk by faith, not by sight."

> Now faith is the substance of things hoped for, the evidence of things not seen.
> But without faith it is impossible to please Him: for he that cometh to God must believe that He is, and that He is a rewarder of them that diligently seek Him (Heb. 11:1, 6).

Does that mean that we are relegated to an ocean of opinion, where the shores of truth are beyond reach? No. Pilate may have believed there was no hope of knowing *the* truth, but that is precisely what Christ came to announce:

> "Are you king then?" asked Pilate.
> "You've said it, I am king. To this end was I born, and for this cause I came into the world, *that I should bear witness unto the truth. Every one that is of the truth hears my voice.*"[8]

The fact that we can only walk by faith and not by sight does not give us an excuse to walk in the wrong direction, neither does it mean that it makes no difference where we walk (so to speak). Our faith must be aligned to the truth in order that we might walk aright. If we, in this life, believe a lie with all sincerity, we will still find ourselves "out of place" when we "open our eyes" in eternity. Therefore, it is absolutely necessary for us to make sure that our faith corresponds accurately to God's revealed truth, for it will be the reality of that revealed truth which we will see with our own eyes when we come before the Lord.

THE CASE OF NOAH

Noah's example is particularly interesting in this context. "By faith Noah, being warned of God of things not seen as yet, moved with fear, prepared an ark to the saving of his house . . ." (Heb. 11:7).

In Noah's case, there was *revelation*: "being warned of God." The revelation concerned the reality of the sinful condition of human kind, the impending judgment, and the only way of salvation. There was also Noah's *faith* in that revelation. If Noah's faith had been sincere but misplaced, he might have done everything but build an ark. Could he prove to the world's population that they were under God's judgment which was soon to be executed? Could he prove that rain—which they knew nothing of at that time in human history—would come to destroy the world? No! Neither could he prove it to himself, having yet never seen it. However, Noah was saved because he had a valid faith which moved him to obey what God had told him to do. His faith was proven valid because it accurately reflected the reality that soon came to be seen in the flood. Moreover, if Noah's faith accurately reflected reality, it is only because the content of his faith corresponded to the content of the revelation given him by God.

Did those who perished in the flood have "faith"? Yes! But their "faith" was that there was not going to be a flood. They sincerely believed they would be fine, that there was no need to repent of their way of life. Did they receive revelation? Yes! Through God's spokesman, Noah (2 Peter 2:5), and the conviction of the Holy Spirit (cf. Gen. 6:3). Unfortunately, they ignored God's revelation and chose to believe what they wanted. We know that they drowned with the awful realization that their "faith" did not reflect reality.

The point is that we all walk through life with our beliefs and our faith, but our particular beliefs do not change reality. We can be thankful to God that He has made known to us what that "reality" is, so that we have the opportunity of aligning our faith to reality. If God had not revealed to Noah the reality of the situation and what was about to come, Noah would have had no chance to escape. Likewise, if God had not made known to us the reality of sin, the coming judgment, and the way of salvation, we would all be equally in the dark concerning reality.[9]

TRUTH IS REVEALED IN SCRIPTURE

How has God made the truth known to us? Christ, the Living Word of God, came speaking the truth (John 1:1; Heb. 1:2; 1 John 1:1). Before Him, God spoke through the prophets (Heb. 1:1). Now He has given us His Word, and the Holy Spirit who gives witness to the truth (cf. John 16; 1 John 2:27).

> "All Scripture is God breathed" (2 Tim. 3:16).[10]
> "Thy Word is truth" (John 17:17).
> "For the prophecy came not in old time by the will of man: but holy men of God spake as they were moved by the Holy Spirit" (2 Peter 1:21).

Few evangelicals put into question the fact that God has given us His revelation. However, what is often put in question is the *clarity* and *perspicuity*[11] of Scripture. "Yes," they say, "truth has been given. But it is beyond us to ever come to a *sure* interpretation of that revealed truth."

THE INTERPRETATION BARRIER

The whole approach to Scripture in evangelicalism is becoming more and more relative, more view-centered, and increasingly tending to dialogue and debate.[12] It is not rare to find books like <u>Five Views of Sanctification</u>[13] and <u>Four Views on Hell</u>.[14] Doctrine is merely relegated to a world of views. Theological journals are replete with articles advancing one view over another, written by authors taking part "in theological debate." Others are dialoguing with liberals or Catholics. Some colleges and seminaries are advocating the "smorgasbord" approach in which the teacher lays out before students various theological views without taking a position as to what the Scriptures teach. This is all done in the name of humility, as Colson seems to suggest when he says, "The sin of presumption is consuming. It's amazing how much time people spend judging those whose views or church traditions might differ from their own."[15]

What is wrong with such an approach? After all, are we not all fallible? How can we claim to have the correct interpretation? Are we not relegated to a world of views, detached from tangible certainty? How can we speak with authority when so many others do not see it as we do? Is it not presumptuous to think that we are right and others are wrong?

Of course, we are all fallible, and, of course, pride may tempt our hearts. That is why we will all answer before the Judgment Seat of Christ (2 Cor. 5). (We also do well to remember James 3:1 which states that there is a greater judgment on those who teach God's Word.) However, to relegate Scripture's teaching and sound doctrine to matters of debate is to take away from the clarity and authority of Scripture!

Imagine reading this from your Bible:

> Paul, a servant of God . . . for the faith of the saints and for the sharing of my belief system, which rests on, according to my present understanding, the hope of eternal life, apparently promised before all times by the God who does not lie, who has manifested several options of what to believe, some better than others, according to what I have understood and communicated by God's call. . . .
> (1:4) To Titus, my true child in a common faith: Grace and peace from God the Father and Christ Jesus our Savior. . . . (1:7) For the overseer must be above reproach as God's steward, not self-willed, . . . (1:9) Fully convinced in his own mind as to what he has studied, so that he be able to debate well according to his theology, to challenge the thoughts of those who do not hold his particular view. For there are many, especially of the circumcision, who will not hold your views, who come from different perspectives, who need to be at least exposed to your view. They do cause a stir among your people since your people buy their books and support their radio programs. But that is not all bad, since it broadens the mind of your people and exposes them to other views. . . .
> (2:1) For you, share your view according to your perspective; suggest that the older men be temperate, dignified, sensible . . .
> (2:15) Share your thoughts on the above, and challenge people to think about them, with a full realization that you are only

able to speak from your vantage point. Let no one despise you in your way of seeing things. . . .

(3:8) The above is my perspective and I want you to debate and dialogue concerning these things that those who believe in God might learn from one another and do good. That is what I believe is good and useful to men. But do avoid foolish discussions and dialogue with those who are exclusive and dogmatic, because those sessions of talk do not get anywhere.[16]

Sounds like a humble approach, right? Lest I corrupt your minds totally with what is NOT Scripture, please take time and read what the Word of God truly says:

Paul, a servant of God, and an apostle of Jesus Christ, according to the faith of God's elect, and the *acknowledging of the truth* which is after godliness; in hope of eternal life, which God, *who cannot lie*, promised before the world began; but hath in due times *manifested His Word through preaching*, which is committed unto me according to the commandment of God our Saviour;

(1:4) To Titus, mine own son after the common faith. . . .

(1:7) For a bishop must be blameless . . . (1:9) *Holding fast the faithful Word* as he hath been taught, that he may be able by *sound doctrine* both to *exhort* and to *convince* the gainsayers. For there are many unruly and vain talkers and deceivers, specially they of the circumcision: whose *mouths must be stopped*, who subvert whole houses, teaching things which they ought not, for filthy lucre's sake. One of themselves, even a prophet of their own, said, "The Cretians are always *liars*, evil beasts, slow bellies." This witness is *true*. Wherefore *rebuke them sharply, that they may be sound in the faith.* . . .

(2:1) But speak thou the things which become *sound doctrine*: that the aged men be sober-minded, grave, temperate, *sound in faith.* . . .

(2:15) *These things speak, and exhort, and rebuke with all authority.* Let no man despise thee. . . .

(3:8) This is a *faithful saying*, and these things I will that thou *affirm constantly*, that they which have believed in God might be careful to maintain good works. These things are good and profitable unto men. But avoid foolish questions, and genealogies, and contentions, and strivings about the law; for they are unprofitable and vain. . . .[17]

A LESSON FROM TITUS

In his epistle to Titus, Paul speaks of truth and gives us the way to approach the concept of truth. Paul wastes no time in dealing with his subject, mentioning it right in his opening salutation (v.1). He was an apostle in view of the faith of God's elect and the knowledge of the truth.

Why speak of truth to Titus? Because Titus was ministering among a people who were known for their lies. "Cretes are always liars" one of their poets said (cf. 1:12), and Paul acknowledged the truthfulness of that saying. In fact, just as the Corinthians were known fornicators, the Cretes were known liars. Just as the world of that time made up the verb "Corinthianize" to speak of "fornicating like the Corinthians," they also made up the verb "Cretize" to speak of lying like a Crete.[18]   Thus Paul felt compelled to stress the importance of truth to the one who was to help set up many churches in that area (1:5).

Why speak about truth? Another reason for Paul to speak about truth was that godliness was at stake. Truth and godliness go together. As Paul says from the start, "the acknowledgment of the truth *which is according to godliness*" (NKJV, emphasis added). Sound doctrine makes very practical and relevant demands on how we live. In Titus 2:1, Paul says, "Speak thou the things which become sound doctrine." In that context, the ladies were to conduct themselves in a certain way in order for the Word of God not to be blasphemed (2:5). Servants were to have a conduct that would "adorn the doctrine of God our Savior in all things" (2:10). The truth of God's grace teaches us how to live godly (2:11).

Furthermore, it is by taking heed to the Word of God that the young man cleanses his way (Ps. 119:9). It is by the truthful Word of God that we are to be sanctified (John 17:17). When Adam and Eve followed a lie and turned away from the truth of what God had told them, they became anything but godly. Truth—and truth living—is the necessary ingredient to godliness. Bad doctrine and false teaching will always lead away from godliness.

Thus in writing to Titus, Paul addresses the subject of truth, and the demands it makes on our lives.

Titus was faced with those who taught views contrary to what Paul had taught him (cf. Tit. 1:11, 14). Titus may have had the same questions that haunt many of us today:

> *What is truth?* How do we approach the concept of revealed truth in a turbulent world of a billion changing opinions, of various views, of theological confusion, of scholarly debates which put in question the very foundation of certainty and of knowledge, of religious and theological dialogues between various worlds of belief who seek to learn from one another, rather than from the source of all truth?

> We would soon be *disillusioned* in all of our theological reading. What to believe? Does it make a difference? Every possible view is out there! We are encompassed about by a turbulent sea and by every wind of doctrine (Eph. 4:14). Do we have any authority in exhorting and contradicting others?

> Can I only attain a particular view of truth, and not truth itself? Am I relegated to a world of opinion, and truth is beyond, impossible to know? Why proclaim something unsure? If all I can preach is my opinion, what I *think* is truth, what good does that do? How can we be confident? Why speak at all? Why invest my life, for only propagating theories?[19]

Then amidst the fog of our own potential disillusioned thinking, Paul's voice rings out clearly, dispelling all confusion. With finality, Paul exclaims:

> "TRUTH has been revealed!" (cf. Tit. 1:1-3)
> "TRUTH has been entrusted to me! And I have proclaimed it!" (cf. Tit. 1:3)
> "Now TRUTH is entrusted to you! You proclaim it, boldly, with authority, rebuking those who contradict it! And live it out since 'real' truth leads to godliness!" (cf. Tit. 1:9; 2:7-8; 2:15)[20]

Paul's first point concerning truth is that it has been proclaimed (revealed). Paul himself was the recipient of it (Tit. 1:3). That is why he could speak authoritatively. Of course, we all expect Paul to have spoken authoritatively, since after all, was he not an apostle? However, the revelation of truth and sound doctrine did not stop with the apostles, for they proclaimed and *transmitted* it.[21] That is why Paul could charge Titus to set up pastors who held fast "the faithful word" (Tit. 1:9). These pastors, who had no apostolic authority, were to exhort and convict those who contradicted. They were to do this on the grounds of sound doctrine (Tit. 1:9). And as much as we are still in the church dispensation, Paul's commands to the church leaders and Bible teachers are *directly* applicable to us today.

The point is, there *is* sound doctrine. The wide variety of "Christian" teaching around the globe does not invalidate the fact that there is a body of sound doctrine, nor does it invalidate what this body of sound doctrine teaches.

You might ask, "What is sound doctrine? Whose view of sound doctrine should we accept?" Though it is certain that no two answers here below will ever be exactly the same, the fact remains that each of our personal "infidelities" to the body of revealed truth does not negate its existence, or its perspicuity.

TRUTH IS ACCESSIBLE

The body of revealed truth is accessible and understandable to us through the Scriptures. When Paul taught in Berea on one of his missionary trips, the Bereans were able to verify whether his teaching was accurate. How? By looking into Scripture.[22] Acts 17:11 says:

> [The Bereans] were more noble-minded than those in Thessalonica; they received the word with all readiness, each day searching the Scriptures to see whether these things were so.[23]

If the Scriptures were basically inaccessible to the Bereans because of the limitations of their fallen minds, then they would not have been able to verify the accuracy of Paul's message.

Furthermore, if the truths of Scripture are inaccessible to us because of the limitations of our fallen minds, then why would God have given us His revelation? Why would He also hold us accountable to it?[24]

To argue for the perspicuity of Scripture is not the same as arguing for the fact that we have perfect minds. Of course not! But at the same time, it is not valid to conclude, on the basis that we have fallen minds and imperfect reasoning patterns, that the truths of Scripture are inaccessible to us. To suggest such leaves us locked into a world of relativity with no chance to find solid ground.

WHAT ABOUT THE HARD SAYINGS?

Are there not hard things to understand in the Scriptures? If Scripture is that clear and perspicuous, why is there so much disagreement about the meaning of various passages? The Bible answers these questions by emphatically reaffirming the clarity and perspicuity of the Scriptures:

> Wherefore, beloved, seeing that ye look for such things, be diligent that ye may be found of him in peace, without spot, and blameless. And account that the longsuffering of our Lord is salvation; even as our beloved brother Paul also according to the wisdom given unto him hath written unto you; as also in all his epistles, speaking in them of these things; *in which are some things hard to be understood, which they that are unlearned and unstable wrest, as they do also the other Scriptures, unto their own destruction* (2 Peter 3:14-16, emphasis added).[25]

Yes, there are some hard things to understand, and, yes, there will always be those who misunderstand and misinterpret the Scripture (who is not guilty of that to some degree?). However, Peter is speaking here particularly of those who have a *pattern* of twisting the meaning of the Scriptures in general, not of those whose basic system of Bible interpretation (hermeneutics) is sound.

So why be troubled if there are diverse views on certain teachings of the Scripture? God said it would happen. The fact that there are diverse views does not show that the Scripture is unclear. If Peter could reaffirm Scripture's clarity and perspicuity while talking about the more difficult Pauline passages, how much more can we affirm, proclaim, and emphasize that all His Word is understandable, accessible, and undebatable!

DEBATE: AN INVALID APPROACH TO BIBLICAL TRUTH

Does one debate what is evident? The very use and connotation of the term means that subjects debated are relegated to the realm of the uncertain. This is most evident by the term "debatable," which is said to mean "open to dispute: questionable."[26]

Even if "debate" is taken in its better sense as "to contend in words by considering opposed arguments,"[27] its connotation is far from that of proclamation. The connotation of "proclamation" is that of certainty, of authority. Proclamation and preaching go hand in hand with authority; they are synonymous with declaration and necessitate exposing and rebuking error.

Through the Scriptures, God gives us the responsibility to proclaim sound doctrine, to preach and teach His Word. Paul himself sought to preach Christ, warning every man (Col. 1:28). He told Timothy to "preach the Word; be instant in season and out of season" (2 Tim. 4:2). He wanted pastors to be able to exhort and convict those who contradicted (Tit. 1:9). He told Titus to "rebuke them sharply, that they may be sound in the faith" (Tit. 1:13). He wanted all of us to "speak the truth in love" in contrast to being "children tossed to and fro and carried about with every wind of doctrine" (Eph. 4:14-15). Jude commanded that we all "contend for the faith once delivered" (Jude 3). From these passages, we can see that we are not ordered to simply "discuss" various views regarding God's Word, but rather we are commanded to proclaim it.

The use of the debate medium for theological study inherently attacks the principle of biblical perspicuity. When either a book or a teacher offers two or more views on a certain biblical teaching, without ever taking position on what the Bible says, invariably the biblical material relating to the issues discussed is portrayed as confusing, unclear, and ultimately inaccessible to our understanding. In a theological debate, when there is no conclusion given, what is communicated is that the Scripture is not clear enough to compel any particular conclusion. This in turn inherently takes away from the *importance* of that issue or doctrine, since it is believed that on that issue, the Bible is unclear.[28]

Some may say that the debate approach should be used only with finer points of doctrine. However, what they do not realize is that once the debate approach is adopted as a general rule for understanding theology, there is nothing that safeguards any doctrine from being found "debatable." On any point of doctrine, someone will invariably come along with differing views and will open the "debate."

In fact, that is exactly what is taking place in the evangelical theological arena. I find it particularly alarming to see that the current trend in evangelicalism is to debate even the most basic points of Christian doctrine. From books such as <u>Five Views of Sanctification</u> and <u>Four Views on Hell</u>, we have finally arrived at the ultimate: <u>Four Views on Salvation in a Pluralistic World</u>.[29] The book description is as follows:

> In this book, four perspectives are presented by their major proponents: Normative Pluralism, Inclusivism, Salvation in Christ, and Salvation in Christ alone. This book allows each contributor to present his case and critique the other contributors.[30]

What else is there to debate? Nothing is sacred, and nothing is spared. We are now debating what is at the core of Christianity. The slippery slope of the debate approach would have us exchange the certainty of biblical salvation for the debatable and tentative opinions of theologians. It allows one to put into question the very foundation of Christianity, an unwavering and firm foundation of certainty that the Scriptures would proclaim. We are merely left with views and nothing more to affirm.

Take also, as an example, Erickson's article, "The Fate of Those Who Never Hear."[31] In it he states at length how much is affected by "the debate" on this issue. As he shows, this issue determines one's view on a number of doctrinal points, such as the incarnation, the Trinity, God's character, biblical authority, salvation, truth and logic, hermeneutics, and the nature of religion. Recent controversy has brought forth the questioning of certain teachings, such as Christ's uniqueness and exclusiveness and the necessity of having faith in Him. Because of this, he calls for a careful investigation on "the question of who will be saved, and on what basis."[32] On one hand, his call for more investigation—which I take to mean a serious study of Scripture—is praiseworthy. On the other hand, however, two key words repeatedly used in his article keep the issues within the sphere of human opinion. These two words are "discussion" and "debate."

He has chosen those two terms to describe the context in which these crucial subjects are treated. These terms go along very well with his observed "rethinking" of various evangelical doctrines, and the "raising of questions" on points of Bible doctrine.[33] "Some believe this." "Some believe that." The whole article, showing how many things are being questioned and rethought, reminds me much of Paul's expression "tossed to and fro and carried about with every wind of doctrine" (Eph. 4:14-15).[34]

Therefore, I deplore the fact that the question of "who will be saved, and on what basis?" is reduced to the matter of a debate! Some will argue for one thing, others for another, in the setting of a debate, a forum of human theological opinion regarding God's Word. Have we forgotten then that God's Word gives the answer and gives it clearly and with authority? Are these matters of "life and death" only a matter of debate? What about the injunctions to "preach the Word" and to "contend for the faith once delivered to the saints" (Jude 3)? Are the "certain men crept in unawares," these "ungodly men" (Jude 4), only fellow Christians with another opinion who equally should have a word to say about what is Christianity? Is anyone allowed to set aside these injunctions in order to play the neutral role of a moderator? Yet this is precisely what Erickson is doing in his article; it is precisely what the editors of books presenting various views are doing; it is exactly what a teacher does when he simply presents various views. Therefore, let us reject the debate approach.

DIALOGUE: THE SEARCH FOR "TRUTH"

If the debate medium is inappropriate for matters of biblical revelation, how much less dialogue? Yet more and more evangelicals are calling for dialogue between those of greatly diverging beliefs within and sometimes without Christendom.

Inherent in dialoguing is the recognition that both parties are coming as equals for the benefit of both sides and for mutual learning on the issues that divide both parties. To illustrate the meaning and connotation of the term, let me simply cite the following:

> It is also interesting—indeed revealing—to notice how the terminology used in ecumenical circles changed during a

very short period. The Mexico City meeting of 1963 still employed the 'old' concept of 'witness': "the *witness* of Christians *to* men of other faiths." A year later, at an East Asian Christian conference in Bangkok, the word *witness* was dropped; the theme was "The Christian *encounter with* men of other beliefs." Three years later, in Sri Lanka, the word *encounter* was also dropped. The theme now ran "Christians in *dialogue with* men of other faiths." Throughout, however, the major participants are still identified as *Christians* who dialogue *with* others. In 1970, in Ajaltoun (Lebanon) this was also dropped; the theme was "Dialogue *between* men of living faiths." (The women were apparently still outside of the dialoguers' field of vision!) In 1977, in Chiang Mai, Thailand, the theme was: "Dialogue in Community."[35]

The Evangelical-Roman Catholic Dialogue on Mission (ERCDOM), lead by John Stott and others, well illustrates my contention concerning dialogue. In the introduction of their report, the editors explain that ERCDOM was a dialogue which had the aim of "exchanging theological views in order to increase mutual understanding and to discover what theological ground"[36] was held in common.

> It was not conceived as a step toward Church unity negotiations. Rather it has been a search for such common ground as might be discovered between Evangelicals and Roman Catholics as they each try to be more faithful in their obedience to mission. It was also undertaken quite consciously in the knowledge that there are still both disagreements and misrepresentations between Evangelicals and Roman Catholics which harm our witness to the gospel, contradict our Lord's prayer for the unity of his followers, and need if possible to be overcome.
>
> During the three meetings friendships were formed, a mutual respect and understanding grew, as the participants learned to listen to one another and to grapple with difficult and divisive questions, as well as rejoicing in the discovery of some common understandings.
>
> It was a demanding experience as well as a rewarding one. It was marked by a will to speak the truth, plainly, without equivocation, and in love. Neither compromise nor

the quest for lowest denominators had a place; a patient search for truth and a respect for each other's integrity did.
. . .
The participants in ERCDOM offer this Report to other Evangelicals and Roman Catholics as a sign of their conviction that fidelity to Jesus Christ today requires that we take his will for his followers with a new seriousness. He prayed for the truth, holiness, mission and unity of his people. We believe that these dimensions of the Church's renewal belong together. It is with this understanding that we echo his prayer for ourselves and each other . . . (Jn. 17:17-21).[37]

The approach of the evangelicals involved in ERCDOM was not one of proclamation, but rather one of sharing theological views, of dialoguing. Instead of approaching the Catholics with the proclamation of the truth of God's Word—the salvation message Catholics need to hear—the evangelicals came "searching for truth" and "searching for common ground." In the process of dialoguing, the evangelicals did share with the Catholics. But they did not share *the truth*, only *their view* of truth. That is how inclusive evangelicals turn sound doctrine into human opinion, divesting it of any authority.

That is precisely the saddest part because though these evangelicals have the *right* opinion regarding salvation, they only believe it is their *opinion* and thus are willing to acknowledge the validity of contrary opinions. Therefore, in one sense, these evangelicals have the right opinion, yet in a greater sense, they do *not* have the right opinion because they have *added* to their "right opinion" the opinion that the gospel is large enough for "contrary opinions." It is simply a form of theological relativism.

Why was there such a dialogue between Catholics and evangelicals? Though its participants claimed it was not for the purpose of church unity, nor to find the lowest common denominator, they did admit going into the dialogue with the recognition of mutually being "followers of Christ" and seeing if differences could possibly be overcome. They said:

There are still both disagreements and misrepresentations between Evangelicals and Roman Catholics which harm our witness to the gospel, contradict our Lord's prayer for the unity of his followers, and need if possible to be overcome.[38]

CONSEQUENCES OF A SHIFTED APPROACH TO TRUTH

The result of this debate and dialogue approach is that no one is left with enough authority to identify heresy. The only thing one can do is say, "I think my view is right, but who really knows in the end?" Underlying such a statement is the thought, "We need clearer revelation."

Imagine Noah's family arguing about the proper interpretation of what was revealed to him. Shem says the boat is only figurative for a mental preparation toward an excess of dew that is to come some time later. Japheth holds that the rain is only symbolic of various distresses that will come upon the world. Ham is agnostic and wants the "squabbling" to cease. Noah rebukes them all and begins building the ark, though his wife reproaches his literal fanaticism: "Its leading you to ridiculous actions, like building a boat where there is no water! And you cannot even be sure you have properly understood what the Lord told you!"

We would do well to remember the downfall of many conventions, schools, and organizations, in the early part of this century. Was it not when they began to permit doctrinal and interpretive latitude, when they began to approach the Scriptures as basically unclear, and when they saw Bible content as permitting differing yet equally valid interpretations, that they considered liberal teachers as only those who held to another view? In the liberal-fundamental controversy, they saw the doctrinal "squabbling" only as an internal "debate" between Christians over interpretive issues. They did not see the controversy as Christians *contending* for *the faith* against apostates.

The inclusive conservatives argued that liberals simply had "another view" of Christianity. They thought something like, "Who are we to say they are not in fellowship with God? We cannot contradict them, we are but human." In so doing, they denied that God had given them enough revelation to know the truth.

What did our fundamental forefathers fight for? For doctrine? Yes, but much more than for doctrine. They fought for holding to Scripture as a clear, understandable, and authoritative body of TRUTH! They fought for a biblical approach to truth! They were not simply in a theological debate with liberals; they were proclaiming the faith of the Scriptures!

Unfortunately, many of the second generation of fundamentalists rejected the fundamentalist's unpopular stance within society. So they started a new movement, which they called "New-evangelicalism." This movement was one of debate and dialogue, one of learned scholars in philosophy and science. The trends and characteristics they chose to follow were spelled out in an article that probed the minds of the leading evangelicals of that day. Many "currents of thought" of the New-evangelical movement had to do with being theologically open-minded:

- A willingness to re-examine beliefs concerning the work of the Holy Spirit.
- A more tolerant attitude toward varying views on eschatology.
- A re-opening of the subject of biblical inspiration.
- A growing willingness of evangelical theologians to converse with liberal theologians.[39]

Not only was there a recognizable shift from "truth-centered" theology to a more "view-centered" theology in such a milieu, but dialogue became the cherished way of "reaching out." As Vernon Grounds states in the article:

> An evangelical can be organizationally separated from all Christ-denying fellowship and yet profitably engage in an exchange of ideas with men who are not evangelicals. Why not? How else can we bring them into an experience with the Christ Who is Truth incarnate?[40]

Is dialogue, or the "exchange of ideas" medium, God's intended way to reach the lost? No, but rather, it is by "the foolishness of *preaching*" (1 Cor. 1:21; cf. Rom. 1:15-16).[41] It is not by *exchanging* **ideas** but by *proclaiming* **truth** that we are to win the world for Christ. Why would the lost opt for our ideas rather then their own if all we have are but ideas? It is truth they need, and truth will set them free (John 8:31-32).[42]

Is it any surprise that today main leaders of the evangelical movement such as Colson, Packer, and Stott argue that Catholics simply have another view of the gospel? What began as a subtle shift of approach in the 1950s, led to a movement that has ultimately relativized the very gospel that it claimed to uphold.[43] Packer has voiced the growing current thought of evangelicalism: "What brings salvation, after all, is not *any theory* about faith in Christ, justification, and the church, but faith itself in Christ himself."[44]

Is the Word of God unclear about salvation? Is it unclear regarding justification? Is it debatable regarding the gospel? Is the doctrine of justification only one's view? Is the doctrine of the atonement only mere theory? Inclusivism would answer "Yes" to all of this. Unfortunately, it would relegate us to a world of opinion, where we could never have the certitude of knowing *the* truth regarding the specifics of the gospel. Without plainly stating it, inclusive evangelicals deny that the revelation of God is comprehensible to us in what it says about salvation and how to obtain it.

Just as the secular man advocates belief in relativity because he denies the existence of absolutes, the secularized evangelical advocates *theological relativity* because he denies the *perspicuity of biblically revealed absolutes*. Some evangelicals go even further and simply reject the fact that there are absolutes or that there is such a thing as "*the* truth." However, whether you deny that the Scriptures are clear or deny that they give absolutes, what you are left with is an impotent relativism.

Such impotent relativism makes no authoritative demands on the lives and morals of its adherents. Everyone can do what is right in his own eyes (cf. Judges 21:25; Prov. 16:25). Is it purely coincidence then that there is less and less of a difference between the world and evangelical Christians in matters of moral conduct? A shift in morals is evident according to author and professor James Hunter of the University of Virginia:

> Many of the distinctions separating Christian conduct from "worldly conduct" have been challenged if not altogether undermined. Even the words *worldly* and *worldliness* have, within a generation, lost most of their traditional meaning.[45]

As evangelical theology becomes more and more "view-centered" rather than "truth-centered," we must anticipate a continuing decline in righteous living. Relativism will lead no one to live up to the high standards of godliness. Digressing in a forum of exchanged views will not compel anyone to change his conduct. Only the proclamation of the truth will call for true godliness (see Titus 2:11).

THE BIBLICAL APPROACH

What then is the proper approach to truth? As with Paul, we must believe that the revelation of truth has been given in the pages of Scripture and that this revelation is written in terms capable of being properly understood. The Scriptures, however, also emphasize our need to be diligent in our study. As Paul said to Timothy, "Make every effort to present yourself approved to God, a worker who needs not be ashamed, rightly dividing the word of truth."[46] Knowing what the Scriptures teach is not gained in flippant study. Diligence, carefulness, and reliance upon the Spirit of God need to be carried out when searching the pages of Scripture.[47]

Just as the Bereans were diligent to verify the accuracy of Paul's teaching, we as well are responsible to think through critically what we hear and read concerning the Bible. We are to prove all things, holding fast what is good and abstaining from every form of evil (1 Thess. 5:21, 22). I trust you will do just that, even as you read this book.

For those who are put in the place of teaching the Scriptures, the responsibility is much greater and will be followed by a greater judgment (James 3:1). The responsibility is to proclaim the Word, to say, "Thus sayeth the Lord." It is to do basically as the Levites did in Nehemiah's day: "So they read in the book in the law of God distinctly, and gave the sense, and caused them to understand the reading" (Neh. 8:8).

Bible preaching and Bible exposition are not antithetical to a reasoned approach. Peter says to be ready, in all meekness, to give reason of the hope that lies within us to anyone who asks (1 Peter 3:15). In like manner, we should be able to give clear and adequate reasons for the teaching we give concerning Scripture.

Furthermore, Paul taught Titus and Timothy not to back down to those who contradicted. He taught them to stay with their message and to keep proclaiming the Word of God with all authority. They were not to diminish the Word of God into mere opinion.

On the other hand, they were also not to make their own opinion the Word of God. In Jeremiah 23, God specifically condemns the false prophets for doing such:

> Thus saith the LORD of hosts, "Do not listen to the words of the prophets who prophesy unto you: they make you vain. They speak a vision of their own heart, not from the mouth of the LORD. They continually say unto them that despise me, 'The LORD hath said, "Ye shall have peace". . . . ' I have not sent these prophets, yet they ran. I have not spoken to them, yet they prophesied. . . . I have heard what the prophets said, that prophesy lies in My Name, saying, 'I have dreamed, I have dreamed.' How long shall this be in the heart of the prophets that prophesy lies? Yea, they are prophets of *the deceit of their own heart*, who think to cause My people to forget My Name by their dreams. . . . The prophet who has a dream, let him tell a dream; and he who has My Word, let him speak My Word faithfully. What is the chaff to the wheat?" saith the LORD. "Is not My Word like as a fire?" saith the LORD; "and like a hammer that breaks the rock in pieces?" (v. 16-29, *ad passim*)[48]

Proverbs 30:5-6 says:

> Every word of God *is* pure; He *is* a shield unto them that put their trust in Him. Do not add to His words, lest He reprove you, and you be found a liar (NKJV).

Therefore, Jeremiah and Proverbs warn us *not* to say, "Thus saith the Lord," when He has *not* spoken, while Titus teaches us *not to refuse* to say, "Thus saith the Lord" when He *has* indeed spoken!

Finally, we must never forget that the proclamation of the Word goes hand in hand with godliness. It is not sufficient for us to declare what the Bible says. We must also live it out, so that we, through our conduct,

> . . . may adorn the doctrine of God our Savior in all things. For the grace of God that brings salvation has appeared to all men, teaching us that, denying ungodliness and worldly lusts, we should live soberly, righteously, and godly in the present age, looking for the blessed hope and glorious appearing of our great God and Savior Jesus Christ, who gave Himself for

us, that He might redeem us from every lawless deed and purify for Himself *His* own special people, zealous for good works (Titus 2:10-14 NKJV).

At His coming, we will answer to Him for how we have handled the Word of life (2 Cor. 4-5; 2 Tim. 2:15).

CONCLUSION

"What is truth?" While the echo of the question resounds in the dark corners of many hearts today, the answer is given clearly in the pages of Scripture. Just as Noah was warned of what was to come, we are also given revelation of the reality of things unseen. By faith in that revealed truth, we will be able to walk in a way that will not make us ashamed when we come before God.

While some people do away with absolutes by denying their existence, others reject them by locking them up behind interpretive barriers. Either way, relativity is erected in the place of absolutes.

Our responsibility to live according to the Word of God starts with how we approach the concept of truth. If we hold that His revelation was not clear enough for us to define properly the faith for which to contend, we will not be able to obey His injunction to contend for the faith once delivered to the saints. Everyone and anyone will be welcome, as long as he has "faith"—however he defines it.

Therefore, compelled by the claims of Scripture themselves, we must come to the Scripture as *the* truth which sets us free and which sanctifies us unto God (John 8:32; 17:17).

NOTES ON CHAPTER 4

1. Quoted by Larry D. Pettegrew "Liberation Theology and Hermeneutical Preunderstandings" in *Bibliotheca Sacra* (July, 1991): 285, from Wayne A. Grudem, "A Response to Contextualization and Revelational Epistemology," in <u>Hermeneutics, Inerrancy, and the Bible</u>, ed. Earl D. Radmacher and Robert D. Preus (Grand Rapids: Zondervan Publishing House, 1984), 755-56, emphasis original.

2. Philip D. Kenneson, "There's Not Such Thing as Objective Truth, and It's a Good Thing, Too," in <u>Christian Apologetics in the Postmodern World</u>, ed. Timothy R. Phillips and Dennis L. Okholm (Downers Grove, Ill.: InterVarsity Press, 1995), 155-70, as quoted by R. Albert Mohler, Jr., " 'Evangelical': What's in a Name?" in <u>The Coming Evangelical Crisis</u>, ed. John H. Armstrong (Chicago: Moody Press, 1996), 38.

3. J. Richard Middleton and Brian J. Walsh, <u>Truth is Stranger Than It Used to Be: Biblical Faith in a Postmodern Age</u> (Downers Grove, Ill.: InterVarsity Press, 1995), 4-5, as quoted by Mohler, 37.

4. W. Gary Phillips, "Evangelical Pluralism: A Singular Problem," *Bibliotheca Sacra* (April-June 1994): 142.

5. Norman Geisler wrote an excellent article on the nature of truth [Norman L. Geisler, "The Concept of Truth in the Inerrancy Debate," *Bibliotheca Sacra* (Oct., 1980): 327-339]. In his article, he presents two views of truth: one is the non-correspondence view of truth, or as he calls it in the context of his article, the intentionality view of truth. He says, "According to this view a statement is true if 'it accomplishes what the author intended it to accomplish,' and conversely, a statement is false if it does not" (p. 328). Let us read a paragraph written by Geisler on Berkouwer to illustrate such a view:

    > Berkouwer makes it clear he holds this same intentionalist or functional view of truth. He wrote approvingly of Kuyper that "he was not at all troubled by the absence of accuracy and exactness precisely because of the God-breathed character of Scripture: the reliability of the Gospels was guaranteed by this purpose of the Spirit" (G. C. Berkouwer, *Holy Scripture*, Studies in Dogmatics, comp. and ed. Jack B. Rogers [Grand Rapids: Wm. B. Eerdmans Publishing Co., 1975], p. 250, italics added). Berkouwer also stated, "The authority of Scripture is in no way diminished because an ancient world view occurs in it; for it was not the *purpose* of Scripture to offer revealing information on that level" (ibid., p. 181). [Geisler, 328, footnote 10]

    The second view is the correspondence view of truth. "According to this view, truth is 'that which corresponds to the actual state of affairs,' to the way things really are. If this theory of truth is correct, then an 'error' is that which does not correspond with the facts, with what is really the case" [Geisler, 328].

    He goes on to show that the Scripture's use of the term "truth" consistently reflects the "correspondence theory of truth." He says:

    > . . . one view of truth is broad enough to include the other, but not the reverse. For example, a true statement will always accomplish its intention, but what accomplishes its intention is not always true. Lies and falsehood sometimes accomplish their intentions

too. Hence only the correspondence view is adequate as a *comprehensive* view of truth. Further, if truth is only personal but not propositional, there is no adequate way of explaining the numerous biblical passages where truth means propositional correspondence. [Geisler, 332, emphasis original]

He also points out that "the biblical use of the word err does not support the intentional theory of truth, since it is used of unintentional 'errors' (cf. Lev. 4:2, 27; etc.)" [Geisler, 334].

6. Phillips, 142. He also went on to say:

Likewise such absolutism is tolerated as acceptable and coherent in the discipline of analytical philosophy. However (and inconsistently), the concept of absolute truth seems to grate on modern ears when applied to spiritual truth-claims. The same relativist who moves away from an oncoming train expresses moral outrage when evangelicals assert the absolutist claim that Jesus is the Way, the Truth, and the Life. Relativism is intolerant of what it perceives as intolerance ["Evangelical Pluralism: A Singular Problem," *Bibliotheca Sacra* (April-June 1994): 142].

7. The temptation to revert to pluralism's relative-truth view is also felt keenly by the inclusivists. Millard Erickson, in discussing the impact of the inclusivist position on various doctrines relates:

This problem also bears on the nature of truth and of logic. An earlier view of truth held that the truth of a proposition also means the falsehood of its contradiction. One way to refute a statement was to verify its contradictory. Conversely, arguing for the truth of a proposition might require refuting what contradicted it. This was because logic was believed to apply.

This position encounters some difficulty in the current discussions on salvation. Traditionally Christianity and its competitors, the other major world religions, have been seen as contradicting each other in sufficiently significant ways so that both could not be simultaneously true in the same respect. If, however, contemporary pluralism is correct, these apparently contradictory views are actually the same thing. To say this, however, requires one of two tactics. One would require a criticism of one or both of the religions, concluding that they do not teach what they have been thought to teach, or if they do teach that, people are not bound to accept that teaching. The other tactic would be to revise logic, so that two statements can actually contradict each other, and yet both be true. On this basis, the locus of truth would not be objectively within the propositional statements, but subjective or in terms of the effect produced in the person exposed to them [Erickson, "The Fate of Those Who Never Hear," 3-15].

8. John 18:37-38, slightly adapted for continuous dialogue, emphasis added.

9. Regarding faith and the content of one's faith, John MacArthur makes some striking comments in his book, Reckless Faith (Wheaton, IL: Crossway Books, 1994):

... pluralism and diversity have been enshrined as higher virtues than truth itself. We're not supposed to say our beliefs are right and all others are wrong. That is regarded as backward, outmoded, discourteous. In other words, we're not really supposed to *believe* our religious beliefs; we're only allowed to hold them as personal preferences.

Evangelicalism is beginning to absorb that latitudinarianism. Not that most evangelicals would accept Islam, Hinduism, or other overtly non-Christian religions. But many seem to think it doesn't really matter what you believe, as long as you label it Christianity. With the exception of a few cults that blatantly renounce the Trinity, almost everything taught in the name of Christ is accepted by evangelicals—from Roman Catholicism (which denies that sinners are justified solely by faith) to the extreme charismatic Word Faith movement (which both corrupts the doctrine of Christ and makes temporal health and wealth the focus of salvation).

> In the name of unity, such matters of doctrine are expressly *not* supposed to be contested. We are being encouraged to insist on nothing more than a simple affirmation of faith in Jesus. Beyond that, the specific *content* of faith is supposed to be a matter of individual preference [p. 92-93].

10. Author's translation.

11. Perspicuity is said of that which is perspicuous, that is "plain to the understanding especially because of clarity and precision of presentation" [Webster's 9th New Collegiate Dictionary].

12. A sobering matter to consider is the call for dialogue. This is sounded out even by some who opposed the implications of ECT: e.g. Agustin B. Vencer Jr., "An International Perspective on Evangelical-Catholic Cooperation," *Evangelical Missions Quarterly* (July 1995): 278-279. See also Ralph R. Covell, "The Christian Gospel and World Religions: How much Have American Evangelicals Changed?" *International Bulletin of Missionary Research* (January 1991): 12-16; Timothy George (senior editor), "Catholics and Evangelicals in the Trenches," *Christianity Today* (May 16, 1994): 16-17; and Kantzer, "Should Roman Catholics and Evangelicals Join Ranks?" *Christianity Today* (July 18, 1994): 17.

13. Melvin E. Dieter, Anthony A. Hoekema, et al., Five Views of Sanctification (Grand Rapids: Zondervan Publishing House, 1987).

14. William V. Crockett, ed., Four Views on Hell (Grand Rapids: Zondervan Publishing, 1996). Other examples: Wayne A. Grudem, ed., Are Miraculous Gifts for Today? Four Views (Grand Rapids: Zondervan Publishing, n.d.); Five Views on Law and Gospel (Grand Rapids: Zondervan Publishing, 1996); Andrew Jukes, ed., Four Views of Christ (n.p.: Kregel Publications, 1993); Gleason L. Archer, ed., Three Views on the Rapture (Grand Rapids: Zondervan Publishing, 1996); Robert G. Clouse and Bonnidell Clouse, eds., Women in Ministry-Four Views (n.p.: Intervarsity Press, 1989); Dennis L. Okholm and Timothy R. Phillips, eds., Four Views on Salvation in a Pluralistic World (Grand Rapids: Zondervan Publishing, 1996).

15. Chuck Colson, The Body (Dallas: Word Publishing, 1992), 88.

16. This is *not* a version of the Bible. The biblical text was purposely changed for the purpose of the argument.

17. Titus, *ad passim*, emphasis added.

18. R. C. H. Lenski, "Titus," in The Interpretation of St. Paul's Epistles: Colossians - Philemon (Minneapolis: Augsburg Publishing House, 1964), 903.

19. Taken from author's sermon, May 1997, Central Baptist Theological Seminary, Minneapolis, MN.

20. Paraphrased and condensed for sake of emphasis.

21. I am not arguing that the giving of [new] revelation continued on past the apostles and the prophets, but that the revelation that was given to them is also given to us through their writings [the N.T.].

22. The Scripture that was then revealed, in other words, the Old Testament Scripture.

23. Author's translation.

24. Regarding accountability, it is interesting to consider what Christ told the Pharisees in John 5:45-47:

    Do not think that I will accuse you to the Father: there is *one* that accuseth you, *even* Moses, in whom ye trust. For had ye believed Moses, ye would have believed me: for he wrote of me. But if ye believe not his writings, how shall ye believe my words?

    We who have received His written revelation will be judged according to that revelation. Our accountability will have to do with the light which we have received, and for us who have received the light of God's Word, that light is great! See also John 12:47-49.

25. Cf. Mat. 13:13-15.

26. Webster's 9th New Collegiate Dictionary.

27. Ibid.

28. This is true, even if the participants in the debate approach Scripture appropriately, arguing that the Scriptures are clear in what they teach and that each person is responsible to God to follow that clear teaching on whatever subject. For though the presentations of the participants might be good in terms of how they personally approach truth, these types of presentations are given *in the context of a debate*, in the general context of neutrality. Both participants are given equal time and in a sense, given equal credibility. This invariably casts shadows of uncertainty, and argues subtly yet powerfully that the teachings of Scripture on the given subject are not clear enough to justify taking a dogmatic position.

29. Dennis L. Okholm and Timothy R. Phillips, eds., Four Views on Salvation in a Pluralistic World (Grand Rapids: Zondervan Publishing, 1996).

30. Taken from the World Wide Web, at URL: <http://www.trinityzone.com/trinity/product.asp?sku=0310212766> (current version 8 Oct 1998).

31. *Bibliotheca Sacra* (January-March 1995): 3-15.

32. Ibid.

33. Here is a sample to give the flavor of the article:

    "The 19th century opened this issue to *debate*. . . ."

    "These *discussions* are spurring new *debates* regarding the necessity of evangelism."

    "The *debate* is important also because of much wider issues. . . ."

    "Groups as conservative as the Evangelical Theological Society are *riven by debate* regarding these matters, with Clark Pinnock, John Sanders, and others taking more inclusivist positions."

"Some consider that God's omniscience . . . and, even more, His justice need to be *rethought.*"

"Sometimes a related question is *raised* . . ."

"This *calls into question* His omnipotence."

"All this challenges believers to *rethink* their stance toward missions."

" . . . they do suggest the need for *rethinking* its grounds."

"Another and more obvious point of effect of the *discussion* relates to the nature of salvation. What is the nature of salvation? What does it mean to be saved? This *raises* a whole complex of issues in contemporary thought."

"The nature of salvation relates to divine justice, and thus the matter is in need of *further discussion.*"

"Thus the whole question of the nature of religion, whether it is an autonomous sphere of human experience, or whether it can be assimilated into some other type of experience, becomes part of the agenda generated by this *discussion.*"

"There also is a need for this *discussion* because of the large amount of attention given to this topic in recent years" [p. 3-15, *ad passim*, emphasis added].

34. In fairness to Erickson's article, I realize it is the first article of a series on those issues, and his goal for the first issue was to present the issues, and the importance of treating these issues. However, the matter in which he chose to do it, by considering these crucial issues in terms of discussion and debate, and by taking on the "neutral" role of simply stating what some believe on this and what others believe on that, puts into question the clarity of Scripture on the given points. Instead, an author wanting to introduce an issue which would be developed subsequently can introduce the problems that are raised by various teachings on the issue, and declare what shape his defense of the relevant biblical teaching will take. In such a way, he remains faithful to the Biblical injunction for him to "preach the Word" and to refute error.

35. David J. Bosh, "The Church in Dialogue: From Self-Delusion to Vulnerability," *Missiology: an International Review* (16:2, April 1988): 134.

36. Meeking and Stott (eds), The Evangelical-Roman Catholic Dialogue on Mission, 1977-1984. A report (Exeter: Paternoster, 1986), 10-11.

37. Ibid., 10-12.

38. Ibid.

39. Editorial, "Is Evangelical Theology Changing," *Christian Life* (March, 1956): 13-16. Illustrating the debate approach that was claimed to be taken in the new movement, here is one paragraph:

But for the last ten years debate has been raging on these subjects. . . . One theologian expressed to CHRISTIAN LIFE fear that conservative Christianity might be seriously split between "those who wish to identify their views with strict orthodoxy and those who wish to keep eschatology as a matter of open and free discussion." But among theologians, at least, the "free and open" spirit is winning out.

Last year's debate on the tribulation between Harold John Ockenga of Boston's Park Street Church and John Walvoord of Dallas Theological Seminary in the pages of CHRISTIAN LIFE is an example. It caused a flurry of comment pro and con. Yet generally it was accepted as a legitimate discussion for an evangelical magazine [p. 15].

40. Ibid., 16.

41. The sufficiency of the preaching of God's Word seems to have been put into question by the early New-evangelical leaders when these wanted, as they put it, "an increased emphasis on scholarship":

> Says Cornelius Van Til of Westminster Seminary: "To present the full implication of the Gospel requires a body of men who are trained in the sciences and in philosophy and who fathom the significance of the Christian religion for these fields." . . . It's clear that evangelicals do not glory in ignorance. *The evangelical scholar does not stab a finger at the Bible and say, "This is it, take it or go to hell."* As Warren C. Young of Northern Baptist Theological Seminary puts it: "The evangelical believes that his position can be supported and justified by a *scholarly consideration* of the case. He is the apologist for conservative Christianity" [Ibid., 15].

Although it is definitely important to be able to "give reason of the hope that is within us" (1 Pet. 3:15), Paul states that we are not to try to present Christ from the framework of secular philosophy and human wisdom (1 Cor. 1:18-21).

42. From a pragmatic consideration, has Vernon Grounds' suggestion to dialogue with liberals in order to win them worked? Not from what can be seen (nor would it have made it right). In fact, it is not the liberals that have come closer to the truth, but rather the evangelical movement that has moved away from it. So agree the reports given in such books as The Coming Evangelical Crisis (John Armstrong, ed), The Great Evangelical Disaster (by Francis Schaeffer), No Place for Truth or Whatever Happened to Evangelical Theology? (by David Wells) written by evangelicals on their own movement.

43. In fact, early New-evangelicals often claimed to limit their concern to the essentials (the gospel): "The fundamentalist watchword is 'Ye should earnestly contend for the faith.' The Evangelical emphasis is 'Ye must be born again' " ["Is Evangelical Theology Changing," 14].

44. Packer, "Why I Signed It," *Christianity Today* (December 12, 1994): 37, emphasis added.

45. Hunter, Evangelicalism: The Coming Generation, 63.

46. 2 Tim. 2:15, author's translation.

47. It is the Spirit that permits us to understand what God has revealed to us in His Word (1 Cor. 2:9ff). Our prayer should be like that of the Psalmist: "Open thou mine eyes, that I may behold wondrous things out of thy law" (Ps. 119:18). 2 Timothy 2:7 says, "Consider what I say; and the Lord give thee understanding in all things," and thus balances our responsibility to rely on the Spirit with our responsibility to actively use our minds in considering what the Word of God says.

48. Author's translation, based on the KJV.

Chapter 5

THE GOSPEL AND THE FUNDAMENTALS OF CHRISTIANITY

Whosoever transgresseth, and abideth not in the doctrine of Christ, hath not God. He that abideth in the doctrine of Christ, he hath both the Father and the Son.

— 2 John 9

I T IS QUITE A DAUNTING TASK to write, even so briefly, on the subject of the gospel. Any time one speaks out as God's spokesman is sobering enough, but it is even more sobering to speak concerning the gospel since the gospel is a matter of life and death. A false gospel is damning, while the true gospel is the power of God unto salvation (Rom. 1:16; cf. Gal. 1:8-9).

It is not that the gospel is complicated. It is in essence very simple. How many of us were born again when we were young? I, myself, was saved when I was but five years old. I simply believed the gospel in its simplicity. I believed that I was a sinner and needed to be saved, that God gave His Son Jesus who died for me so that I did not have to pay for my own sins, that He lives and that He could save me and forgive my sins. That day, I knew that I had become a child of God, because Jesus died for me, and that day I was transformed, having the Holy Spirit to change me and sanctify me.

Did I know everything about the doctrine of salvation? Did I know the glorious details of such a wonderful gospel? Of course not. I have since grown much in that knowledge, but even at that young age, through my simple faith in Jesus, I was a child of God and will be His child forever. No matter how much we discuss the gospel, we always need to keep in mind its simplicity.

But to say the gospel is simple does not mean that it need not be defined. To the contrary! If God had not defined the gospel in His Word, what hope would we have to know our destiny? The Bible itself has repeatedly defined the gospel, and we dare not ignore its teachings!

The definition of the gospel is closely linked to any consideration of the fundamentals of Christianity. The *gospel* is the message we proclaim for someone to become Christian; it focuses primarily on what a lost person needs to know in order to come to Christ. The *fundamentals* of the faith are all the doctrines of biblical teaching which are essential to Christianity, and without all of which there would be no genuine Christianity. There is a great overlap between the gospel and the fundamentals, and for all practical purposes the terms will be used as synonymous in this chapter.[1] It might also be necessary to speak of the *essentials* of Christianity which would include both the fundamental doctrines of Christianity and the "fundamental practices" of Christianity. I am referring by this latter term to sanctification, which is essential, both in doctrine and in practice, to genuine Christianity (see Heb. 12:14; we will deal with sanctification in the body of this chapter). The *essentials* of the Christian faith differentiate true Christianity from false Christianity; they set apart those who truly know God from those who do not.

Before looking at the biblical data, let us first review what some inclusive evangelicals have suggested as to the essential message of Christianity. Erickson had said:

Perhaps, in other words, it is possible to receive the benefit of Christ's death without conscious knowledge-belief in the name of Jesus. What, then, is the essential nature of the gospel message? Several elements are involved: (1) The belief in one good powerful God. (2) The belief that he (man) owes this God perfect obedience to his law. (3) The consciousness that he does not meet this standard, and therefore is guilty and condemned. (4) The belief that God is merciful, and will forgive and accept those who cast themselves upon his mercy.[2]

Colson gave a core set of beliefs which he called the "rule of faith":

> • God the creator exists in three persons, Father, Son and Holy Spirit.
> • Born of the virgin, He suffered, died, rose again, and was exalted at the right hand of the Father from whence He will come again.
> • The Holy Spirit brings the benefits of Christ's saving work to people who believe in Him.
> • Christians are expected to unite with a local church, submit to the authority of bishops and elders, live a holy life conducive to the spread of the gospel.
> • God will judge the world and receive His own at the end of history.[3]

He also added to that list "something that the first-century church took for granted: belief in the authority of God's inerrant Word."[4] Later in his book, Colson also listed five fundamentals, which he says are the non-negotiables of the faith:

1. The infallibility of Scripture
2. The deity of Christ
3. The Virgin Birth and miracles of Christ
4. Christ's substitutionary death
5. Christ's physical resurrection and eventual return.

These were then, as they are today, the backbone of orthodox Christianity. If a fundamentalist is a person who affirms these truths, then there are fundamentalists in every denomination—Catholic, Presbyterian, Baptist, Brethren, Methodist, Episcopal. . . . Everyone who believes in the

orthodox truths about Jesus Christ—in short, every
Christian—is a fundamentalist. [5]

The question is, are these definitions sufficient to contrast
between true and false Christianity? It is obvious that Erickson
believes that someone who has never heard of Jesus Christ can be
saved. That means that much of the gospel we preach in evangelical
churches would be totally nonessential. On his side, Colson considers
as truly Christian the orthodox Catholic whose "faith in Christ"
consists of trusting in a system of rituals, sacraments and works to get
him—maybe and hopefully—to heaven.

Is this what the Word of God would have us believe as to the
gospel and fundamentals of Christianity? To answer this question, let
us look at the biblical data and try to understand what the gospel is
and what is revealed as fundamental to the Christian faith.[6]

In looking into Scripture, we will keep in mind two things. First,
we will consider that the Scriptures give us knowledge of what it takes
to become a genuine child of God (2 Tim. 3:15), and what we need to
become mature and complete, "throughly furnished unto all good
works" (2 Tim. 3:17). Therefore, we will need to distinguish between
what it says is necessary to be of *born* of God and what it says is
necessary for the *growth* of the born again.

Second, we will also consider the fact that the Scriptures
prophesied that there would be false teachers who would try to pervert
Christianity (1 Tim. 4:1; 2 Peter 2:1; cf. Gal. 2:4-5).[7] These false
apostles come in the guise of Christian workers (2 Cor. 11:13) while
twisting one point or another of the fundamental doctrines of
Christianity. In dealing with such false teachers, the apostles
clarified, in various passages, certain points of doctrine regarding
what must be believed or what must not be denied in order for
someone to be genuinely a child of God.[8] These passages are
particularly helpful to us in our consideration of the gospel and the
fundamentals of the Christian faith.

CONCERNING SCRIPTURE

The Bible begins by declaring itself essential to anyone's saving faith. Without Scripture, and without receiving it as God's Word, there would be no possibility of salvation or, consequently, of Christianity.[9]

> And that from a child thou hast known the Holy Scriptures, which are able to make thee wise unto salvation through faith which is in Christ Jesus (2 Tim. 3:15).

> The law of the LORD is perfect, converting the soul (Ps. 19:7; see also Ps. 119:9).

> So then faith cometh by hearing, and hearing by the Word of God (Rom. 10:17).

> For this cause also thank we God without ceasing, because, when ye received the Word of God which ye heard of us, ye received it not as the word of men, but as it is in truth, the Word of God, which effectually worketh also in you that believe (1 Thess. 2:13; see also Gal. 1:11-12).

> Being born again, not of corruptible seed, but of incorruptible, by the Word of God, which liveth and abideth for ever. . . . And this is the Word which by the gospel is preached unto you (1 Peter 1:23, 25).[10]

> Of his own will begat he us with the word of truth, that we should be a kind of firstfruits of his creatures (James 1:18).

You cannot dissociate salvation and Christianity from the necessary delivery and acceptance of the Word of God and its message.[11] Lest we should overlook the implications of the passages above, let us read from Georges Peters who counters the claim that there can be true "men of faith" outside of Christianity:

> Regarding so-called "men of faith" in non-Christian religions, two facts need to be emphasized. First, there seems to be a mystic-realistic relationship between saving faith and hearing the Word of God. Faith is born out of hearing the Word. Paul wrote that "faith cometh by *hearing*, and hearing by the word of God" (Rom. 10:17). Similarly he questioned

the Galatians, "Received ye the Spirit by the works of the law, or by the *hearing* of faith?" (Gal. 3:2). This is in keeping with the words of Christ: "No man can come to me, except the Father which hath sent me draw him: . . . It is written in the prophets, and they shall all be taught of God. Every man therefore that hath *heard*, and hath *learned* of the Father, cometh unto me" (John 6:44-45). These passages relate saving faith to hearing the Word of God similar to the way James and Peter relate the new birth to the Word of God (James 1:18; 1 Pet. 1:23). Does one therefore have a right to speak of "men of faith" *apart* from the Word of God? Abraham "staggered not at the *promise* of God . . . being fully persuaded that, what [God] had *promised*, he was able also to perform" (Rom. 4:20-21). The Word of God was the source of Abraham's faith.[12]

This emphasis on the fact that the Scriptures are essential to Christianity correlates well with Christ's centrality in Christian doctrine, for Christ is the incarnate Word (John 1:1, 14). He is called the "Word of life" in 1 John 1:1, and He upholds the absolute authority and trustworthiness of the Written Word (Matt. 5:18).[13] He Himself said:

> Verily, verily, I say unto you, he that *heareth my word*, and believeth on Him that sent me, hath everlasting life, and shall not come into condemnation; but is passed from death unto life (John 5:24, emphasis added).

Christ also said, "If ye *continue in my word*, then are ye my disciples indeed" (John 8:31, emphasis added). Peter said, "Lord, to whom shall we go? Thou hast the words of eternal life" (John 6:68). These words were given to us in the record of the New Testament. And, as Chafer reminds us, "God has caused a record concerning His Son to be written and men who believe that record are saved, and those who do not believe that record are lost (1 John 5:9-12)."[14]

In fact, even this record of the Son, along with the forth-giving of His gospel in the New Testament, is delicately tied to the authority of the Scriptures that God had previously given (the Old Testament). Thus, we see in the New Testament an abundant use of the expression, "according to the [O.T.] Scriptures." Paul's gospel was according to the revelation found in the Scriptures of the prophets (cf.

Rom. 16:24-26). The Old Testament Scriptures witnessed of Christ (Luke 24:27; John 5:39; cf. John 7:38). Paul argued from Scripture that Jesus was the Messiah (Acts 18:28; cf. Acts 8:35). Christ died and rose again according to the Scriptures (Luke 24:25-26, 45-47; John 20:9; 1 Cor. 15:3-4). Scripture foretold the gospel (Rom. 1:1-2) by announcing that salvation to the Gentiles would be by faith (Gal. 3:8; cf. Rom. 10:11). It is the Scriptures that conclude that all are under sin (Gal. 3:22; Rom. 3:10ff).[15] Therefore, even the gospel expounded in the New Testament was established on the authority of what God had previously revealed in the Old Testament.

Thus, we should understand not only that individually we are born again through the Word of God, but also that foundationally even the gospel was given on the basis of the previously revealed Word of God. Remove the Scriptures, and there is nothing left—no gospel or any possibility of regeneration.

The Scriptures are not only necessary to saving faith, but also completely sufficient to produce saving faith. "The law of the LORD is perfect, converting the soul" (Ps. 19:7). Because of the perfection of God's Word, there is no need for anything else. In fact, not only is there no *need* for a supplement to God's Word, but with the Word of God, there is no *room* for any supplement. When traditions are given religious authority alongside Scripture, they nullify the Scriptures. Christ said to the Pharisees:

> Why do you also transgress the commandment of God by your tradition? . . . Thus you have made the commandment of God of no effect by your tradition. Hypocrites! Well did Isaiah prophesy of you, saying,
> "This people draws nigh unto me with their mouth,
> And honors Me with their lips,
> But their heart is far from Me,
> And in vain they do worship Me,
> Teaching as doctrines the commandments of men"
> (Mat. 15:3, 6-9; see also Mark 7:6-13).[16]

Paul warns the Colossians:

> Beware lest anyone cheat you through philosophy and empty deceit, according to the tradition of men, according to the

basic principles of the world, and not according to Christ (Col. 2:8 NKJV).

Therefore, the Scriptures *alone* are able and necessary to establish what is true Christianity. This is precisely what the Reformation sought to re-establish with *Sola Scriptura* (Scripture alone).

If spiritual life can come only through the knowledge given in the Scriptures and the acceptance of its teachings as coming from God, we ought not to be surprised that a rejection of God's Word brings doom, as the prophet Isaiah tells us:

> Therefore as the fire devoureth the stubble, and the flame consumeth the chaff, so their root shall be as rottenness, and their blossom shall go up as dust: because *they have cast away the law* of the LORD of hosts, and *despised the Word* of the Holy One of Israel (Isa. 5:24, emphasis added).[17]

CONCERNING THE TRIUNE GOD

The Scriptures go on to explain clearly the belief that must be held concerning God. To begin with, faith is necessary: "The just shall live by faith" (Rom. 1:17) and "without faith, it is impossible to please [God]" (Heb. 11:6). However, God is not talking of just any kind of faith: "for he that cometh to God must believe that He is, and that He is a rewarder of them that diligently seek Him" (Heb. 11:6b). This faith is essentially the recognition that God exists, and that He is a good and personal Being with whom it is possible to have a relationship.[18] A New Age belief in a mystical nonpersonal god is antithetical to Christianity.

[a]First John 5:20, John 14:6, and Acts 4:12 affirm that salvation comes exclusively through the knowledge of the true God through Jesus Christ (see also John 17:3; 20:31; 1 John 5:9-10). Furthermore,

---

[a]1 John 5:20   "And we know that the Son of God is come, and hath given us an understanding, that we may know him that is true, and we are in him that is true, *even* in his Son Jesus Christ. This is the true God, and eternal life."

John 14:6   "Jesus saith unto him, I am the way, the truth, and the life: no man cometh unto the Father, but by me."

Acts 4:12   "Neither is there salvation in any other: for there is none other name under heaven given among men, whereby we must be saved."

it is stated in no uncertain terms that belief in the deity of Christ is essential to our being of God [b](1 John 4:15; cf. John 8:58; 10:30). Belief that Jesus was the Messiah and that He was truly incarnate is also necessary [c](1 John 4:2-3; 5:1). In that light, belief in the biblically revealed virgin birth of Christ safeguards the doctrine concerning Christ's dual nature (see Mat. 1:23; Luke 1:35). It is the person of Christ, His deity and His humanity, that permitted Him to be the propitiation for our sins on the cross. We will discuss more on His work below.

Regarding the Trinity, 1 John 2:23 says, "Whosoever denieth the Son, the same hath not the Father: but he that acknowledgeth the Son hath the Father also." (see John 5:23). A recognition of the third person of the Trinity, the Spirit of God, is also inherent to a true child of God since it is the Spirit who regenerates and bears "witness with our spirit that we are children of God" (Rom. 8:16; Gal. 4:6). "Hereby know we that we dwell in Him, and He in us, because He hath given us of His Spirit" (1 John 4:13). We know that the Spirit comes from the Father, is sent by Christ (John 15:26), and speaks of Christ (John 16:13-14; see 1 Cor. 12:3; 16:22).

CONCERNING SALVATION

The Scriptures are also explicit about how God has provided salvation. This salvation is in the work of Christ at Calvary. "Christ is the end of the law for righteousness to everyone who believeth" (Rom. 10:4). Christ's prophesied name is "The Lord our righteousness" (Jer. 23:6; 33:16) because God made Him who knew no sin to be sin for us "that we might be made the righteousness of God in Him" (2 Cor. 5:21; see also 1 John 3:5). Only love moved the Father to give us His Son, and only love moved Christ to die in the place of sinners (John 3:16; Rom. 5:6,8; Rev. 1:5). God had set Him

---

[b]1 John 4:15   "Whosoever shall confess that Jesus is the Son of God, God dwelleth in him, and he in God."

[c]1 John 4:2-3   "Hereby know ye the Spirit of God: Every spirit that confesseth that Jesus Christ is come in the flesh is of God: And every spirit that confesseth not that Jesus Christ is come in the flesh is not of God. . . . "

1 John 5:1   "Whosoever believeth that Jesus is the Christ is born of God: and every one that loveth him that begat loveth him also that is begotten of him."

forth to be "a propitiation by His blood, through faith, to demonstrate His righteousness . . . , that He might be just and the justifier of the one who has faith in Jesus" (Rom. 3:25-26 NKJV).

Christ's substitutionary death is intrinsic to the gospel (1 Cor. 15:3). Those who deny Christ's once-for-all, finished sacrifice on the cross (Heb. 9:27; Rom. 6:10; cf. John 19:30), are exactly like the foretold false prophets who "deny the Lord that bought them" (2 Peter 2:1). Hebrews 10:29 gives solemn warning:

> Of how much worse punishment, do you suppose, will he be thought worthy who has trampled the Son of God underfoot, counted the blood of the covenant by which he was sanctified a common thing, and insulted the Spirit of grace? (NKJV)

Christ's bodily resurrection is also essential to the gospel. It assures us of eternal life and of victory over death (1 Cor. 15:3, 56-57). "If Christ be not risen, your faith is vain; ye are yet in your sins!" (1 Cor. 15:17). Christ was "delivered for our offenses, and raised for our justification" (Rom. 4:25). As Paul insists in 1 Corinthians 15:2, belief in the death and resurrection of Christ is absolutely necessary.

CONCERNING HOW SALVATION IS OBTAINED

Through the Scriptures, the gospel is also very explicit as to how one can obtain God's salvation. First, a recognition of one's sinful and lost state is necessary. Christ told the Pharisees that unless one recognizes his sinful condition, he has no chance of being forgiven (John 9:39-41; see also Matt. 9:12-13). John affirms that a misunderstanding concerning one's sinfulness is fundamental evidence that one has not the truth. "If we say that we have no sin, we deceive ourselves, and the truth is not in us. . . . If we say that we have not sinned, we make Him a liar, and His Word is not in us" (1 John 1:8-10). These verses may apply to the one who thinks he has arrived at perfection following his professing Christ. They may also apply to the one who denies ever having possessed a sinful nature. Paul defines himself and all the saved as those who, by their trespasses, were once spiritually dead and "by nature the children of wrath," but who have, through faith in Christ, been risen with Christ and seated in the heavens (Eph. 2:1-10). This change from death to life is the new birth Christ spoke about and without which no one will enter the kingdom of God (John 3:3-8). Jesus explained the new birth as the act of placing one's faith in the Son of God (John 3:10-18). Anyone who wants to claim that he has always believed and does not recognize that there was ever a time when he was lost cannot claim to have eternal life or to have passed "from death unto life" as Christ put it (John 5:24).

Second, one must have faith in Christ. Let us consider three aspects concerning faith. To begin with, faith is believing. Those who have come to the point of recognizing their innate sinfulness and lost condition can turn to God in faith and be saved. They must come to God by faith in Christ's finished work alone without any trust in their works (Eph. 2:8-10). Those who believe in Christ are "justified freely by His grace through the redemption that is in Christ Jesus" (Rom. 3:24). Justification through faith alone is plainly defined in Galatians and in Romans:

> . . . knowing that a man is not justified by the works of the law but by faith in Jesus Christ, even we have believed in Christ Jesus, that we might be justified by faith in Christ and not by the works of the law; for by the works of the law no flesh shall be justified. . . . I do not set aside the grace of God; for if righteousness *comes* through the law, then Christ died in vain (Gal. 2:16, 21 NKJV; see also Titus 3:3-7; 1 Peter 1:18-19).

> Now to him who works, the wages are not counted as grace but as debt. But to him who does not work but believes on Him who justifies the ungodly, his faith is accounted for righteousness (Rom. 4:4-5 NKJV).

When Israel sought to establish their own righteousness, they did not submit to the righteousness of God (Rom. 10:3; cf. Is. 64:6). To turn the righteousness of God—which is freely gained (Rom. 3:24; 4:4-5)—into something that is gained progressively in life, through sacraments and righteous living, is to twist the truth unto one's own destruction.

Faith also involves calling upon the Lord:

> That if you confess with your mouth the Lord Jesus and
> believe in your heart that God has raised Him from the dead,
> you will be saved.   For with the heart one believes to
> righteousness, and with the mouth confession is made to
> salvation. For the Scripture says, *"Whoever believes on Him*
> *will not be put to shame."* For there is no distinction between
> Jew and Greek, for the same Lord over all is rich to all who
> call upon Him.   For *"whoever calls upon the name of the*
> *LORD shall be saved."* How then shall they call on Him in
> whom they have not believed? (Rom. 10:9-14a NKJV)

In this passage, calling on the Lord is linked with faith. We must
remember that it is not prayer or words spoken, but faith that saves.[19]
Calling on the Lord expresses the faith of the one coming to Christ.
True faith *will* express itself and will confess as Paul indicates above.

Furthermore, faith includes repentance. No one can be saved
unless he has done the will of the Father (Matt. 7:21) which is that
"no one should perish, but that all should come to repentance" (2
Peter 3:9). Paul preached to the Athenians that God now commands
"all men every where to repent" (Acts 17:30).[20]

> The necessity of repentance as a condition of salvation is
> clearly indicated on the biblical witness. . . . The demand for
> repentance in the witness of Jesus and of the apostles as well
> as the fact that repentance is unto the remission of sins and
> eternal life . . . show that there is no salvation apart from
> repentance. This does not interfere with the complimentary
> truth that we are saved through faith. . . .[21]

Repentance and faith are like two sides of a coin. Both are part of the
message that we should proclaim around the world. Christ announced
"that repentance and remission of sins should be preached in His name
among all nations, beginning at Jerusalem" (Luke 24:47).   Paul
testified "both to the Jews, and also to the Greeks, *repentance* toward
God, and *faith* toward our Lord Jesus Christ" (Acts 20:21, emphasis
added).

Repentance is the recognition of one's sinful and lost condition
before a holy God, and consists of the change of mind and heart from
not believing, to believing in Christ. It invariably involves turning to

God while repudiating what one used to trust, serve and live for. Hebrews 6:1 speaks of "repentance from dead works, and faith toward God." The Thessalonians "turned to God from idols to serve the living and true God, and to wait for His Son from heaven, whom He raised from the dead, even Jesus, which delivered us from the wrath to come" (1 Thess. 1:9-10; see also Heb. 9:28; Phil. 3:20; cf. 1 John 3:2,3; Titus 2:13). When Cornelius and his household heard the gospel and believed, Peter and the rest of the Jews recognized that God had granted to them also "repentance unto life" (Acts 11:18). As 2 Corinthians 7:10 tells us, "For godly sorrow worketh repentance to salvation not to be repented of: but the sorrow of the world worketh death."

Concerning Sanctification and Perseverance

Sanctification is also inherent to Christianity (cf. Heb. 12:14). Holiness and good works, coupled with true doctrine, serve as evidence of knowing God. Faith that leaves a person totally unchanged is non-genuine and unbiblical; it is not saving faith. Biblical faith is always followed by sanctification and a changed life, to some degree—not to perfection during this life, as 1 John 1:8,10 declares (cf. 2 Cor. 5:17ff).

> If we say that we have fellowship with Him, and walk in darkness, we lie and do not [practice] the truth. . . . And hereby we do know that we know him, if we keep His commandments. He that saith, I know Him, and keepeth not His commandments, is a liar, and the truth is not in him (1 John 1:6; 2:3-4).

> For as the body without the spirit is dead, so faith without works is dead also (James 2:26; see 2:14-26).

Furthermore, the one who returns into the world and renounces his "faith" only demonstrates that there was no substance to his believing. Similar is the case of one who professes the gospel but later believes in an altered gospel, a "gospel" that denies one or several points fundamental to Christianity. For example, let us consider 1 Corinthians 15:1-2. Paul was confident in the true and lasting nature of the Corinthians' faith (v.1). However, he stated hypothetically that if they turned away from believing in the resurrection, they would reveal that their original belief was of no genuine essence (vain) and that they were never genuinely saved. True faith endures and does not turn away from the truth of the gospel, while an empty faith does not last. This in essence is the doctrine of the perseverance of the saints (see also 1 John 2:19).

Other passages bring this out clearly. For instance, Christ said, "If ye continue in my word, then are ye my disciples indeed" (John 8:31). Paul says something similar to the Colossians: "And you . . . hath he reconciled . . . if ye continue in the faith grounded and settled, and be not moved away from the hope of the gospel" (Col. 1:21, 23). The point is, Paul does not say they *will be* reconciled (in the future) if they continue, but they *have been* reconciled (in the past) if they remain grounded and steadfast in the hope of the gospel. Someone who falls away reveals that he was never genuinely reconciled unto God. Willard M. Aldrich puts it succinctly:

> "Whose house are we, if we hold fast the confidence and the rejoicing of the hope firm unto the end," [Heb. 3:6] and conversely, we are not His house now, if we do not hold fast unto the end.
>
> "You he reconciled, if ye continue in the faith," [Col. 1:21-23] and conversely, you were not reconciled, if you do not continue in the faith.
>
> "We have become partakers of Christ, if we hold the beginning of our confidence stedfast unto the end" (Heb. 3:14), and conversely, we have not become partakers of Christ unless we hold stedfast unto the end.
>
> These passages do not teach that we can be saved and lost again, but they serve as tests of whether we have ever been saved. They are in harmony with the implications of the statement made by Christ to professing but unsaved Christians who had wrought miracles in His name, "I never knew you: depart from me, ye that work iniquity" (Matt. 7:23). His statement precludes the possibility of their having been saved and lost again. "Not at any time have I known you."[22]

Scripture is thus emphatic that true Christianity has a live and enduring faith that draws one closer to the image of God's Son (Col.

3:10; cf. 2 Cor. 3:18). The Scriptures do not say that at the first sin, a Christian should wonder if he has adequately believed. The righteous fall yet rise up again (Prov. 24:16). The genuine Christian will know that he is Christ's through the witness of the Spirit that indwells him (Rom. 8:16). Therefore when he sins, he is convicted, and can confess and be forgiven, knowing that he has "an advocate with the Father, Jesus Christ the righteous" (1 John 2:1).

God ensures the sanctification of his genuine children through His chastening, in order that we "might be partakers of His holiness" (Heb. 12:10). As Hebrews 12:7-8 tells us:

> If you endure chastening, God deals with you as with sons; for what son is there whom a father does not chasten? But if you are without chastening, of which all have become partakers, then you are illegitimate and not sons (NKJV).

Therefore, for a professing believer who goes back into the world, it is difficult to know whether he is being a rebellious child whom God will chasten, or if he was never genuinely saved. Even so, the principle remains that sanctification is inherent to true Christianity.

A WORD OF CAUTION

If the Scriptures establish essentials of the faith, that is not to say that the rest of Bible doctrines are not important. We must beware of setting up a great divide between essential doctrines and the rest of Scripture. Paul taught the whole counsel of God (Acts 20:27), and we need to teach it today also. "All Scripture is God-breathed, and is profitable for doctrine, for reproof, for correction, for instruction in righteousness, that the man of God may be complete, thoroughly equipped for every good work" (2 Tim. 3:16-17).[23]

When the New-evangelical movement was born, it sought to limit its emphasis to the gospel over and against doctrinal matters. It distinguished itself from the fundamentalist movement by stating, *"The fundamentalist watchword is 'Ye should earnestly contend for the faith.' The evangelical emphasis is 'Ye must be born again.'"*[24] Now, a few decades later, the New-evangelical movement has progressively opened itself up to various unscriptural definitions of the new birth. Therefore, the best defense against apostasy is the teaching of all the doctrines of God's Word and the necessity to defend them.

Yet the Scriptures do give us a mandate to discern what is and what is not true Christianity, and therefore we are expected to know what the fundamentals of the faith are. The apostle John said, "Beloved, believe not every spirit, but try the spirits whether they are of God: because many false prophets are gone out into the world" (1 John 4:1). We know that these false apostles portray themselves as being ministers of Christ (2 Cor. 11:13-14), and therefore, the need for vigilance regarding the Christian faith is all the more accentuated.

We must always remember what the apostle John declared: "Whoever goes beyond and does not abide in the doctrine of Christ does not have God. The one who abides in the doctrine, this one has the Father and the Son" (2 John 9).[25]

It is for this doctrine, the doctrine of Christ, for which we must contend. We must warn against both those who explicitly deny any one of the fundamental doctrines (e.g., the Catholics and the liberals) and those who implicitly deny them by rendering them unessential to the Christian faith. In either case, the doctrines of Christ are twisted and corrupted, and what is left is a subverted gospel.

If the Scriptures declare that a doctrine is essential to the gospel, then anyone who claims belief in that doctrine, while denying that it is essential, in reality denies the doctrine. One cannot truly believe in the necessary atonement of Christ if he admits the possibility of someone being saved through some other means. Similarly, one cannot truly believe that salvation is by faith alone if he admits that someone can be saved through infant baptism or other sacraments.

CONCLUSION

Evangelical inclusivism is a deadly paradox. At times in explicit biblical language, it professes to preach and hold to the Christian faith, yet an inclusive gospel, since it is not the true gospel, will never be the power of God unto salvation. It will produce a generation trusting in a "generic core set of beliefs" that does not resemble the true doctrine of Christ. It will slowly squeeze the life out of the evangelical community, divesting it of any authority and godliness, and leaving behind only apostate skeletons holding to nothing more than opinions . . . *unless* evangelicals recognize the error, expose it, repudiate it, and hold fast the Word which was preached to them (1 Cor. 15:2).

Evangelical inclusivism has its heroes, those who advance its cause. They have adopted the *evangelical* epitaph and have even claimed to hold to faith alone. As a sad testimony to their success, these heroes are widely acclaimed in the evangelical community. True born again believers rarely question their genuineness. Even to most fundamentalists, they are considered at worst as "disobedient brethren" for not upholding biblical separation. Rarely are they seen for what they are: wolves in sheep's clothing. Thus, as "insiders," they are in a position to do the most damage. And such they are doing, removing the essentials of the faith and breaking down the walls that distinguish true believers from false ones. They are working toward a unity with liberals, Catholics, and others of contrary beliefs. They are creating a melting pot of religious opinions devoid of any authoritative definitions on the gospel. It is time to reject the work of these "insiders" and expose their evangelical inclusivism as the most subversive enemy of the gospel.

Let the wise hear and beware, let them warn, teach, "exhort, and rebuke with all authority" (Titus 2:15). Let them hear the voice of their Master in the pages of His book, since everyone who is of the truth hears His voice (John 18:37). Let them hold forth the Word of life amidst a crooked and perverse generation (Phil. 2:16). Let them give this Word of life to those who need it: those who have never heard, those who trust in their own goodness, or those who follow after a false gospel.

NOTES ON CHAPTER 5

1. I am not suggesting that the gospel and the fundamentals of the faith are different in essence, only they are different in emphasis. For instance, while the belief in the dual nature of Christ (both divine and human) is essential in Christianity (we will see that later in this chapter), a gospel presentation will not center upon that fact. It will, however, include it at least in passing, while it will press the sinner more directly to recognize his lost condition and to turn to Christ by trusting the finished work of Christ at Calvary. I say "at least in passing" for it would be impossible to share the gospel without communicating the fact that God gave His only Son (speaking of His deity) and that His Son died on the cross, and rose again (speaking of His Humanity). Most people do not have a real problem with those facts, and that is why this particular doctrine is not emphasized in most gospel presentations. However, most people have a much greater difficulty accepting other points of the salvation plan: for instance, on accepting the teaching of the Bible regarding man's sinful and lost condition, and/or on the doctrine of salvation by faith alone (not by works).

2. M. Erickson, "Hope for Those Who Have Never Heard? Yes, But..." *Evangelical Missions Quarterly* (April 1975): 124-125.

3. Colson, <u>The Body</u>, 108, 109.

4. Ibid.

5. Colson draws his list from *The Fundamentals*, a series of volumes on the nonnegotiables of the faith, published between 1910 and 1915 by early fundamentalists in response to the liberal intrusion into their denominations. These did not mean to argue that Catholics and other sacramental denominations were part of orthodox Christianity since they did include "articles defending the doctrine of justification by faith alone, as well as articles titled, 'Is Romanism Christianity?' and 'Rome, the Antagonist of the Nation' " [MacArthur, <u>Reckless Faith</u>, note # 17, p. 235].

6. John MacArthur, in his book <u>Reckless Faith</u>, has a pertinent chapter "What are the Fundamentals of Christianity?" (Chapter 4, pages 91-117) that deals precisely with our subject. He also sees the problem of inclusivism within the evangelical ranks:

   > An aggressive effort is being made to divest "the fundamentals" of key evangelical distinctives. Influential voices within evangelicalism are urging us to pare back the essentials to the barest possible statement of faith, and these voices can be heard across the spectrum of evangelicalism. Appeals for broader tolerance and more inclusivism have come from charismatics, dispensationalists, Calvinists, and Arminians, Reformed and Lutheran leaders—so-called evangelicals of almost every stripe [p. 97].

   He traces generally through history the use of creeds to movements that sought to define more precisely true Christianity in light of various controversies. "Creeds were written to confront error," not to promote unity (p. 99). Instead of turning to creeds to delineate the essential doctrines of Christianity, MacArthur argues that we should go back to Scripture:

> What *are* the doctrines that are truly fundamental, and how do we decide what they are? Can we take them from a creed that was given to us by tradition, not by inspiration? Shouldn't we turn instead to God's Word for instruction about what is really essential to our faith? [p.108].

7. See Robert P. Lightner's excellent article on "A Biblical Perspective on False Doctrine," *Bibliotheca Sacra* (January 1985): 16-22.

8. MacArthur says, "Certain teachings of Scripture carry threats of damnation to those who deny them. Other ideas are expressly stated to be affirmed only by unbelievers. Such doctrines, obviously, involve fundamental articles of genuine Christianity" [MacArthur, Reckless Faith, 112].

9. J. H. Traver says, "The written Word of God is also the means by which man can become spiritually alive (Ps. 119:50), for it is called the 'incorruptible seed' by which man is 'born again' (1 Pet. 1:23). Not only does God use reproduction in the animal realm to illustrate spiritual truth, but He also uses reproduction in the plant realm and describes the Word of God as the 'seed' which God, the sower (Matt. 15:13) sows into infertile and fertile ground (Mark 4:1-20)" [Traver, "The Biology of Salvation," *Bibliotheca Sacra* (July 1963): 257].

10. Peter Davids comments on this passage:

> In the beginning God generated life through his word, a theme repeatedly seen in Gen. 1 (cf. Ps. 33:6, 9; Rom. 4:17) and in John 1:3, but also significantly found in Isa. 40 (especially v. 26, although the whole chapter speaks of the creative and re-creative power of God). Now he regenerates through his word (as in Jas. 1:18), which is here described as "living," that is, "life-giving," "creative," or "effective" (John 6:63; cf. 5:24; Phil. 2:16; Heb. 4:12; cf. Isa. 55:10-11), and "enduring" (Matt. 24:35 . . .).
>
> Thus Scripture itself proves that God's Word, which is the word by which they were reborn, can never be superseded. And, adds Peter, if by any chance he has not been clear, it is this word which was announced as good news when the gospel was preached to them and they were converted [Peter H. Davids, NICNT: The First Epistle of Peter (Grand Rapids: W. B. Eerdmans Pub., 1990), 78, 79].

11. The quoted passages fall on deaf ears when it comes to evangelical inclusivists. Millard Erickson well realizes the implications of inclusivism on Bibliology. He says:

> The traditional understanding of the Bible is that it is the sole authority in matters of faith and practice. If this is the case, then what of those who have no access to the content of the specially revealed truth preserved in the Bible? Some believe that salvation may be possible through "implicit faith," or by responding to what can be known about God and the human predicament from general or natural revelation. If this is the case, then what is the unique status of special revelation? Is it really necessary? [Millard J. Erickson, "The Fate of Those Who Never Hear," *Bibliotheca Sacra* (January-March 1995): 3-15].

For a detailed and biblical rebuttal to this kind of inclusivism, see Ramesh P. Richard, "Soteriological Inclusivism and Dispensationalism," *Bibliotheca*

Sacra (January-March 1994): 85-108. See also his book, <u>The Population of Heaven - A Biblical Response to the inclusivist position on who will be saved</u> (Chicago: Moody Press, 1994).

12. George W. Peters, "Perspectives on the Church's Mission. Part IV: Missions in a Religiously Pluralistic World," *Bibliotheca Sacra* (October-December 1979): 300, emphasis added.

13. It is interesting to note that most often when Christ quoted the Old Testament, He quoted a Greek translation of the Hebrew.

14. Lewis Sperry Chafer, <u>Systematic Theology: Vol. 1, Bibliology</u> (Grand Rapids: Kregel Publications, 1993), 60.

15. See also James 2:23; Romans 4:3.

16. Author's translation.

17. Luke 16:28-31 reminds us that those who reject God's Word are those who reject the most persuasive element God has given to convince. No one who rejects it will be found guiltless. Abraham pointed to nothing else than to "Moses and the Prophets" (Scripture) when the rich man spoke of his brothers' need for repentance and salvation. For it is the Scriptures that lead to life.

18. Leon Morris says:
   First, he must believe that God exists. This is basic. Without it there is no possibility of faith at all. But it is not enough of itself. After all, the demons can know that sort of faith (James 2:19). There must also be a conviction about God's moral character, belief "that he rewards those who earnestly seek him." As Barclay puts it, "We must believe, not only that God exists, but also that God cares" (in Loc.). Without that deep conviction, faith in the biblical sense is not a possibility [Morris, "Hebrews" in the <u>Expositor's Bible Commentary</u>, vol. 12 (Grand Rapids: Zondervan Publishing House, 1981), 115-116].

19. In this context, we must be aware of the dangers of making the often used "sinner's prayer" the way of salvation.

20. See also Matt. 4:17; Luke 13:3, 5; Acts 3:19; 5:31; 11:18; 17:30; 20:21; 2 Tim. 2:25.

21. J. Murray, "Repentance" in <u>New Bible Dictionary</u>, ed. J.D. Douglas (Grand Rapids: Wm. B. Eerdmans Publishing Co., 1962), 1083-1084.

22. Willard M. Aldrich, "Perseverance," *Bibliotheca Sacra* (January, 1958): 18-19.

23. Author's translation

24. "Is Evangelical Theology Changing," 14, emphasis added.

25. Author's translation.

APPENDIX A
ROMAN CATHOLIC MATERIALS
FOR REFERENCE

EXTRACTS FROM: "THE CATECHISM OF THE CATHOLIC CHURCH"

ON RELIGIOUS AUTHORITY

[paragraph 95] "It is clear therefore that, in the supremely wise arrangement of God, sacred Tradition, Sacred Scripture and the Magisterium of the Church are so connected and associated that one of them cannot stand without the others. Working together, each in its own way, under the action of the one Holy Spirit, they all contribute effectively to the salvation of souls."

[100] The task of interpreting the Word of God authentically has been entrusted solely to the Magisterium of the Church, that is, to the Pope and to the bishops in communion with him.

ON THE CHURCH

[168] It is the Church that believes first, and so bears, nourishes and sustains my faith. Everywhere, it is the Church that first confesses the Lord: "Throughout the world the holy Church acclaims you", as we sing in the hymn Te Deum; with her and in her, we are won over and brought to confess: "I believe", "We believe". It is through the Church that we receive faith and new life in Christ by Baptism. In the Rituale Romanum, the minister of Baptism asks the catechumen: "What do you ask of God's Church?" And the answer is: "Faith." "What does faith offer you?" "Eternal life."

[169] Salvation comes from God alone; but because we receive the life of faith through the Church, she is our mother: "We believe the Church as the mother of our new birth, and not in the Church as if she were the author of our salvation." Because she is our mother, she is also our teacher in the faith.

ON SACRAMENTS

[1210] Christ instituted the sacraments of the new law. There are seven: Baptism, Confirmation (or Chrismation), the Eucharist, Penance, the Anointing of the Sick, Holy Orders and Matrimony.

THE SACRAMENT OF BAPTISM

[1213] Holy Baptism is the basis of the whole Christian life, the gateway to life in the Spirit (vitae spiritualis ianua), and the door which gives access to the other sacraments. Through Baptism we are freed from sin and reborn as sons of God; we become members of Christ, are incorporated into the Church and made sharers in her mission: "Baptism is the sacrament of regeneration through water in the word."

[1239] The essential rite of the sacrament follows: Baptism properly speaking. It signifies and actually brings about death to sin and entry into the life of the Most Holy Trinity through configuration to the Paschal mystery of Christ. Baptism is performed in the most expressive way by triple immersion in the baptismal water. However, from ancient times it has also been able to be conferred by pouring the water three times over the candidate's head.

[1250] Born with a fallen human nature and tainted by original sin, children also have need of the new birth in Baptism to be freed from the power of darkness and brought into the realm of the freedom of the children of God, to which all men are called. The sheer gratuitousness of the grace of salvation is particularly manifest in infant Baptism. The Church and the parents would deny a child the priceless grace of becoming a child of God were they not to confer Baptism shortly after birth

[1257] The Lord himself affirms that Baptism is necessary for salvation. He also commands his disciples to proclaim the Gospel to all nations and to baptize them. Baptism is necessary for salvation for those to whom the Gospel has been proclaimed and who have had the possibility of asking for this sacrament. The Church does not know of any means other than Baptism that assures entry into eternal beatitude; this is why she takes care not to neglect the mission she has received from the Lord to see that all who can be baptized are "reborn of water and the Spirit." God has bound salvation to the sacrament of Baptism, but he himself is not bound by his sacraments.

[1260] "Since Christ died for all, and since all men are in fact called to one and the same destiny, which is divine, we must hold that the Holy Spirit offers to all the possibility of being made partakers, in a way known to God, of the Paschal mystery." Every man who is ignorant of the Gospel of Christ and of his Church, but seeks the truth and does the will of God in accordance with his understanding of it, can be saved. It may be supposed that such persons would have desired Baptism explicitly if they had known its necessity. [INCLUSIVE OF THOSE WHO HAVE NEVER HEARD]

[1262] The different effects of Baptism are signified by the perceptible elements of the sacramental rite. Immersion in water symbolizes not only death and purification, but also regeneration and renewal. Thus the two principal effects are purification from sins and new birth in the Holy Spirit.

[1263] By Baptism all sins are forgiven, original sin and all personal sins, as well as all punishment for sin. In those who have been reborn nothing remains that would impede their entry into the Kingdom of God, neither Adam's sin, nor personal sin, nor the consequences of sin, the gravest of which is separation from God.

[1264] Yet certain temporal consequences of sin remain in the baptized, such as suffering, illness, death, and such frailties inherent in life as weaknesses of character, and so on, as well as an inclination to sin that Tradition calls concupiscence, or metaphorically, "the tinder for sin" (fomes peccati); since concupiscence "is left for us to wrestle with, it cannot harm those who do not consent but manfully resist it by the grace of Jesus Christ." Indeed, "an athlete is not crowned unless he competes according to the rules."

[1265] Baptism not only purifies from all sins, but also makes the neophyte "a new creature," an adopted son of God, who has become a "partaker of the divine nature," member of Christ and co-heir with him, and a temple of the Holy Spirit.

[1266] The Most Holy Trinity gives the baptized sanctifying grace, the grace of justification: 1 - enabling them to believe in God, to hope in him, and to love him through the theological virtues; 2 - giving them the power to live and act under the prompting of the Holy Spirit through the gifts of the Holy Spirit; 3 - allowing them to grow in goodness through the moral virtues. Thus the whole organism of the Christian's supernatural life has its roots in Baptism.

THE SACRAMENT OF THE EUCHARIST

[1324] The Eucharist is "the source and summit of the Christian life." "The other sacraments, and indeed all ecclesiastical ministries and works of the apostolate, are bound up with the Eucharist and are oriented toward it. For in the blessed Eucharist is contained the whole spiritual good of the Church, namely Christ himself, our Pasch."

[1325] "The Eucharist is the efficacious sign and sublime cause of that communion in the divine life and that unity of the People of God by which the Church is kept in being. It is the culmination both of God's action sanctifying the world in Christ and of the worship men offer to Christ and through him to the Father in the Holy Spirit."

[1326] Finally, by the Eucharistic celebration we already unite ourselves with the heavenly liturgy and anticipate eternal life, when God will be all in all.

[1365] Because it is the memorial of Christ's Passover, the Eucharist is also a sacrifice. The sacrificial character of the Eucharist is manifested in the very words of institution: "This is my body which is given for you" and "This cup which is poured out for you is the New Covenant in my blood." In the Eucharist Christ gives us the very body which he gave up for us on the cross, the very blood which he "poured out for many for the forgiveness of sins."

[1366] The Eucharist is thus a sacrifice because it re-presents (makes present) the sacrifice of the cross, because it is its memorial and because it applies its fruit: [Christ], our Lord and God, was once and for all to offer himself to God the Father by his death on the altar of the cross, to accomplish there an everlasting redemption. But because his priesthood was not to end with his death, at the Last Supper "on the night when he was betrayed," [he wanted] to leave to his beloved spouse the Church a visible sacrifice (as the nature of man demands) by which the bloody sacrifice which he was to accomplish once for all on the cross would be re-presented, its memory perpetuated until the end of the world, and its salutary power be applied to the forgiveness of the sins we daily commit.

[1371] The Eucharistic sacrifice is also offered for the faithful departed who "have died in Christ but are not yet wholly purified," so that they may be able to enter into the light and peace of Christ: Put this body anywhere! Don't trouble yourselves about it! I simply ask you to remember me at the Lord's altar wherever you are. Then, we pray [in the anaphora] for the holy fathers and bishops who have fallen asleep, and in general for all who have fallen asleep before us, in the belief that it is a great benefit to the souls on whose behalf the supplication is offered, while the holy and tremendous Victim is present. . . . By offering to God our supplications for those who have fallen asleep, if they have sinned, we . . . offer Christ sacrificed for the sins of all, and so render favorable, for them and for us, the God who loves man.

THE SACRAMENT OF CONFIRMATION

[1285] Baptism, the Eucharist, and the sacrament of Confirmation together constitute the "sacraments of Christian initiation," whose unity must be safeguarded. It must be explained to the faithful that the reception of the sacrament of Confirmation is necessary for the completion of baptismal grace. For "by the sacrament of Confirmation, [the baptized] are more perfectly bound to the Church and are enriched with a special strength of the Holy Spirit. Hence they are, as true witnesses of Christ, more strictly obliged to spread and defend the faith by word and deed."

[1310] To receive Confirmation one must be in a state of grace. One should receive the sacrament of Penance in order to be cleansed for the gift of the Holy Spirit. More intense prayer should prepare one to receive the strength and graces of the Holy Spirit with docility and readiness to act.

[These texts are taken from the World Wide Web, at URL:
<http://www.christusrex.org/www1/CDHN/ccc_cont.html> (current version 6 Oct 1997)]

EXTRACT FROM A CATHOLIC STATEMENT ON BIBLICAL FUNDAMENTALISM

[This is an extract from the statement, entitled: *Pastoral Statement for Catholics on Biblical Fundamentalism*. It is from the National Conference of Catholic Bishops Ad Hoc Committee on Biblical Fundamentalism, chaired by Archbishop John Whealon of Hartford, Conn. Statement released Sept. 30 and dated March 26, 1987.]

This is a statement of concern to our Catholic brothers and sisters who may be attracted to biblical fundamentalism without realizing its serious weaknesses. We Catholic bishops, speaking as a special committee of the National Conference of Catholic Bishops, desire to remind our faithful of the fullness of Christianity that God has provided in the Catholic Church.

Fundamentalism indicates a person's general approach to life which is typified by unyielding adherence to rigid doctrinal and ideological positions—an approach that affects the individual's social and political attitudes as well as religious ones.

Fundamentalism in this sense is found in non-Christian religions and can be doctrinal as well as biblical. But in this statement we are speaking only of biblical fundamentalism, presently attractive to some Christians, including some Catholics.

Biblical fundamentalists are those who present the Bible, God's inspired word, as the only necessary source for teaching about Christ and Christian living. This insistence on the teaching Bible is usually accompanied by a spirit that is warm, friendly, and pious. Such a spirit attracts many (especially idealistic young) converts. With ecumenical respect for these communities, we acknowledge their proper emphasis on religion as influencing family life and workplace. The immediate attractions are the ardor of the Christian community and the promises of certitude and of a personal conversion experience to the person of Jesus Christ without the need of church. As Catholic pastors, however, we note its presentation of the Bible as a single rule for living. According to fundamentalism, the Bible alone is sufficient. There is no place for the universal teaching church—including its wisdom, its teachings, creeds, and other doctrinal formulations, its liturgical and devotional traditions. There is simply no claim to a visible, audible, living, teaching authority binding the individual or congregations.

A further characteristic of biblical fundamentalism is that it tends to interpret the Bible as being always without error or as literally true in a way quite different from the Catholic Church's teaching on the inerrancy of the Bible. For some biblical fundamentalists, inerrancy extends even to scientific and historical matters. The Bible is presented without regard for its historical context and development.

In 1943 Pope Pius XII encouraged the church to promote biblical study and renewal, making use of textual criticism. The Catholic Church continued to study the Bible as a valuable guide for Christian living. In 1965 the Second Vatican Council, in its constitution on Divine Revelation, gave specific teaching on the bible. Catholics are taught to see the Bible as God's book—and also as a collection of books written under divine inspiration by many human beings. The Bible is true—and to discover its inspired truth we should study the patterns of thinking and writing used in ancient biblical times. With Vatican II, we believe that "the books of Scripture must be acknowledged as teaching firmly, faithfully and without error that truth which God wanted put into the sacred writings for the sake of our salvation" (Dogmatic Constitution on Divine Revelation, 11). We do not look upon the Bible as an authority for science or history. We see truth in the Bible as not to be reduced solely to literal truth, but also to include salvation truths expressed in varied literary forms.

We observed in biblical fundamentalism an effort to try to find in the Bible all the direct answers for living—though the bible itself nowhere claims such authority. The appeal of such an approach is understandable. Our world is one of war, violence, dishonesty, personal and sexual irresponsibility. Its a world in which people are frightened by the power of the nuclear bomb and the insanity of the arms race, where the only news seems to be bad news. People of all ages yearn for answers. They look for sure, definite rules for living. And they are given answers—simplistic answers to complex issues—in a confident and enthusiastic way in fundamentalist Bible groups.

The appeal is evident for the Catholic young adult or teen-ager—one whose family background may be troubled; who is struggling with life, morality, and religion; whose Catholic education may have been seriously inadequate in the fundamentals of doctrine, the Bible, prayer life, and sacramental living; whose catechetical formation may have been inadequate in presenting the full Catholic traditions and teaching authority. For such a person, the appeal of finding the ANSWER in a devout, studious, prayerful, warm, Bible-quoting class is easy to understand. But the ultimate problem with such fundamentalism is that it can give only a limited number of answers and cannot present those answers, on balance, because it does not have Christ's teaching church nor even an understanding of how the bible originally came to be written, and collected in the sacred canon, or official list of inspired books.

Our Catholic belief is that we know God's revelation in the total Gospel. The Gospel comes to us through the Spirit-guided tradition of the Church and the inspired books: "This sacred tradition, therefore, and Sacred Scripture of both the Old and New Testament are like a mirror in which the pilgrim church one earth looks at God" (Dogmatic Constitution on Divine Revelation,7).

A key question for any Christian is, Does the community of faith which is the Lord's church have a living tradition which presents God's word across the centuries until the Lord comes again? The Catholic answer to this question is an unqualified yes. That answer was expressed most recently in the Constitution on Divine Revelation of the Second Vatican Council. We look to both the church's official teaching and Scripture for guidance in addressing life's problems. It is the official teaching or magisterium that in a special way guides us in matters of belief and morality that have developed after the last word of Scripture was written. The church of Christ teaches in the name of Christ and teaches us concerning the Bible itself.

The basic characteristic of biblical fundamentalism is that it eliminates from Christianity the church as the Lord Jesus founded it. That church is a community of faith, worldwide, with pastoral and teaching authority. This non-church characteristic of biblical fundamentalism, which sees the church as only spiritual, may not at first be clear to some Catholics. From some fundamentalists they will hear nothing offensive to their beliefs, and much of what they hear seems compatible with Catholic Christianity. The difference is often not in what is said—but in what is not said. There is no mention of the historic, authoritative church in continuity with Peter and the other apostles. There is no vision of the church as our mother—a mother who is not just spiritual, but who is visibly ours to teach and guide us in the way of Christ.

Unfortunately, a minority of fundamentalist churches and sects not only put down the Catholic Church as a "man-made organization" with "man-made rules," but indulge in crude anti-Catholic bigotry with which Catholics have long been familiar.

We believe that no Catholic properly catechized in the faith can long live the Christian life without those elements that are had only in the fullness of Christianity: the eucharist and the other six sacraments, the celebration of the word in the liturgical cycle, the veneration of the Blessed Mother and the saints, teaching authority and history linked to Christ, and the demanding social doctrine of the church based on the sacredness of all human life.

. . .

[Taken from the World Wide Web, URL:
<http://www.ewtn.com/library/bishops/biblfund.txt> (current version 7 Sept 1997)]

APPENDIX B
"THE GIFT OF SALVATION" STATEMENT

For God so loved the world that he gave his only Son, that whoever believes in him should not perish but have eternal life. For God sent the Son into the world, not to condemn the world, but that the world might be saved through him. (John 3 :16-17)

We give thanks to God that in recent years many Evangelicals and Catholics, ourselves among them, have been able to express a common faith in Christ and so to acknowledge one another as brothers and sisters in Christ. We confess together one God, the Father, the Son and the Holy Spirit; we confess Jesus Christ the Incarnate Son of God; we affirm the binding authority of Holy Scripture, God's inspired Word; and we acknowledge the Apostles' and Nicene creeds as faithful witnesses to that Word.

The effectiveness of our witness for Christ depends upon the work of the Holy Spirit, who calls and empowers us to confess together the meaning of the salvation promised and accomplished in Christ Jesus our Lord. Through prayer and study of Holy Scripture, and aided by the Church's reflection on the sacred text from earliest times, we have found that, notwithstanding some persistent and serious differences, we can together bear witness to the gift of salvation in Jesus Christ. To this saving gift we now testify, speaking not for, but from and to, our several communities. God created us to manifest his glory and to give us eternal life in fellowship with himself, but our disobedience intervened and brought us under condemnation. As members of the fallen human race, we come into the world estranged from God and in a state of rebellion. This original sin is compounded by our personal acts of sinfulness. The catastrophic consequences of sin are such that we are powerless to restore the ruptured bonds of union with God. Only in the light of what God has done to restore our fellowship with him do we see the full enormity of our loss. The gravity of our plight and the greatness of God's love are brought home to us by the life, suffering, death, and resurrection of Jesus Christ. "God so loved the world that he gave his only Son, that whoever believes in him should not perish but have eternal life" (John 3:16).

God the Creator is also God the Redeemer, offering salvation to the world. "God desires all to be saved and come to a knowledge of the truth" (1 Timothy 2:4). The restoration of communion with God is absolutely dependent upon Jesus Christ, true God and true man, for he is "the one mediator between God and men" (1 Timothy 2:5), and "there is no other name under heaven given among men by which we must be saved" (Acts 4:12). Jesus said, "No one comes to the Father but by me" (John 14:6). He is the holy and righteous one who was put to death for our sins, "the righteous for the unrighteous, that he might bring us to God" (1 Peter 3:18).

The New Testament speaks of salvation in various ways. Salvation is ultimate or eschatological rescue from she and its consequences, the final state of safety and glory to which we are brought in both body and soul. "Since, therefore we are now justified by his blood, much more shall we be saved by him from the wrath of God." "Salvation is nearer to us now than when we first believed" (Romans 5:9; 13:11). Salvation is also a present reality. We are told that "he saved us, not because of deeds done by us in righteousness, but in virtue of his own mercy" (Titus 3:5). The present reality of salvation is an anticipation and foretaste of salvation in its promised fullness.

Always it is clear that the work of redemption has been accomplished by Christ's atoning sacrifice on the cross. "Christ redeemed us from the curse of the law by becoming a curse for us" (Galatians 3:13). Scripture describes the consequences of Christ's redemptive work in several ways, among which are: justification, reconciliation, restoration of friendship with God, and rebirth from above by which we are adopted as children of God and made heirs of the Kingdom. "When the time had fully come, God sent his son, born of a woman, born under law, that we might receive the adoption of sons" (Galatians 4:4-5).

Justification is central to the scriptural account of salvation, and its meaning has been much debated between Protestants and Catholics. We agree that justification is not earned by any good works or merits of our own; it is entirely God's gift, conferred through the Father's sheer graciousness, out of the love that he bears us in his Son, who suffered on our behalf and rose from the dead for our justification. Jesus was "put to death for our trespasses and raised for our justification" (Romans 4:25). In justification, God, on the basis of Christ's righteousness alone, declares us to be no longer his rebellious enemies but his forgiven friends, and by virtue of his declaration it is so.

The New Testament makes it clear that the gift of justification is received through faith. "By grace you have been saved through faith; and this is not your own doing, it is the gift of God" (Ephesians 2:8). By faith, which is also the gift of God, we repent of our sins and freely adhere to the gospel, the good news of God's saving work for us in Christ. By our response of faith to Christ, we enter into the blessings promised by the gospel. Faith is not merely intellectual assent but an act of the whole persons involving the mind, the will, and the affections, issuing in a changed life. We understand that what we here affirm is in agreement with what the Reformation traditions have meant by justification by faith alone *(soda fide)*.

In justification we receive the gift of the Holy Spirit, through whom the love of God is poured forth into our hearts (Romans 5:5). The grace of Christ and the gift of the Spirit received through faith (Galatians 3:14) are experienced and expressed in diverse ways by different Christians and in different Christian traditions, but God's gift is never dependent upon our human experience or our ways of expressing that experience.

While faith is inherently personal, it is not a purely private possession but involves participation in the body of Christ. By baptism we are visibly incorporated into the community of faith and committed to a life of discipleship. "We were buried therefore with him by
baptism into death, so that as Christ was raised from the dead by the glory of the Father, we too might walk in newness of life" (Romans 6:4).

By their faith and baptism, Christians are bound to live according to the law of love in obedience to Jesus Christ the Lord. Scripture calls this the life of holiness, or sanctification. "Since we have these promises, dear friends, let us purify ourselves from everything that contaminates body and spirit, perfecting holiness out of reverence for God" (2 Corinthians 7:1). Sanctification is not fully accomplished at the beginning of our life in Christ, but is progressively furthered as we struggle, with God's grace and help, against adversity and temptation. In this struggle we arc assured that Christ's grace will be sufficient for us, enabling us to persevere to the end. When we fail, we can still turn to God he humble repentance and confidently ask for, and receive, his forgiveness [sic].

We may therefore have assured hope for the eternal life promised to us in Christ. As we have shared in his sufferings, we will share in his final glory. "We shall be like him, for we shall sac him as he is" (1 John 3:2). While we dare not presume upon the grace of God, the promise of God in Christ is utterly reliable, and faith in that promise overcomes anxiety about our eternal future. We are bowed by faith itself to have firm hope, to encourage one another in that hope, and in such hope we rejoice. For believers "through faith are shielded by God's power until the coming of the salvation to be revealed in the last time" (1 Peter 1:5).

Thus it is that as justified sinners we have been saved, we arc being saved, and we will be saved. All this is the gift of God. Faith issues in a confident hope for a new heaven and a new earth in which God's creating and redeeming purposes are gloriously fulfilled. "Therefore God has highly exalted him and bestowed on him the name which is above every name, that at the name of Jesus every knee should bow, in heaven and on earth and under the earth, and every tongue confess that Jesus Christ is Lord, to the glory of God the Father" (Philippians 2:9-11).

As believers we are sent into the world and commissioned to be bearers of the good news, to serve one another in love, to do good to all, and to evangelize everyone everywhere. It is our responsibility and firm resolve to bring to the whole world the tidings of God's love and of the salvation accomplished in our crucified, risen, and returning Lord. Many are in grave peril of being eternally lost because they do not know the way to salvation.

In obedience to the Great Commission of our Lord, we commit ourselves to evangelizing everyone. We must share the fullness of God's saving truth with all, including members of our several communities. Evangelicals must speak the gospel to Catholics and Catholics to Evangelicals, always speaking the truth in love, so that "working hard to maintain the unity of the Spirit in the bond of peace . . . the body of Christ may be built up until we all reach unity in the faith and in the knowledge of the Son of God" (Ephesians 4: 3, 12-13).

Moreover, we defend religious freedom for all. Such freedom is grounded in the dignity of the human person created in the image of God and must be protected also in civil law.

We must not allow our witness as Christians to be compromised by half-hearted discipleship or needlessly divisive disputes. While we rejoice in the unity we have discovered and are confident of the fundamental truths about the gift of salvation we have affirmed, we recognize that there are necessarily interrelated questions that require further and urgent exploration. Among such questions are these: the meaning of baptismal regeneration, the Eucharist, and sacramental grace; the historic uses of the language of justification as it relates to imputed and transformative righteousness; the normative status of justification in relation to all Christian doctrine; the assertion that while justification is by faith alone, the faith that receives salvation is never alone; diverse understandings of merit, reward, purgatory, and indulgences; Marian devotion and the assistance of the saints in the life of salvation; and the possibility of salvation for those who have not been evangelized.

On these and other questions, we recognize that there are also some differences within both the Evangelical and Catholic communities. We are committed to examining these questions further in our continuing conversations. All who truly believe in Jesus Christ are brothers and sisters in the Lord and must not allow their differences, however important, to undermine this great truth, or to deflect them from bearing witness together to God's gift of salvation in Christ. "I appeal to you, brothers, in the name of our Lord Jesus Christ, that all of you agree with one another so that there may be no divisions among you and that you may be perfectly united in mind and thought" (1 Corinthians 1:10).

As Evangelicals who thank God for the heritage of the Reformation and affirm with conviction its classic confessions, as Catholics who are conscientiously faithful to the teaching of the Catholic Church, and as disciples together of the Lord Jesus Christ who recognize our debt to our Christian forebears and our obligations to our contemporaries and those who will come after us, we affirm our unity in the gospel that we have here professed. In our continuing discussions, we seek no unity other than unity in the truth. Only unity in the truth can be pleasing to the Lord and Savior whom we together serve, for he is "the way, the truth, and the life" (John 14:6).

EVANGELICALS
Dr. Gerald L. Bray (Beeson Divinity School)
Dr. Bill Bright (Campus Crusade for Christ)
Dr. Harold O. J. Brown (Trinity Evangelical Divinity School)
Mr. Charles Colson (Prison Fellowship)
Bishop William C. Frey (Episcopal Church)
Dr. Timothy George (Beeson Divinity School)
Dr. Os Guinness (The Trinity Forum)
Dr. Kent R. Hill (Eastern Nazarene College)
The Rev. Max Lucado (Oak Hills Church of Christ,
    San Antonio, Texas)
Dr. T. M. Moore (Chesapeake Theological Seminary)
Dr. Richard Mouw (Fuller Theological Seminary)
Dr. Mark A. Noll (Wheaton College)
Mr. Brian F. O'Connell (Interdev)
Dr. Thomas Oden (Drew University)
Dr. James I. Packer (Regent College, British Columbia)
Dr. Timothy R. Phillips (Wheaton College)
Dr. John Rodgers (Trinity Episcopal School for Ministry)
Dr. John Woodbridge (Trinity Evangelical Divinity School)

ROMAN CATHOLICS
Fr. James J. Buckley (Loyola College in Maryland)
Fr. J. A. Di Noia, O.P. (Dominican House of Studies)
Fr. Avery Dulles, S.J. (Fordham University)
Fr. Thomas Guarino (Seton Hall University)
Dr. Peter Kreeft (Boston College)
Fr. Matthew L. Lamb (Boston College)
Fr. Eugene LaVerdiere, S.S.S. (Emmanuel)
Fr. Francis Martin (John Paul II Institute for Studies on
Marriage and Family)
Mr. Ralph Martin (Renewal Ministries)
Fr. Richard John Neuhaus (Religion and Public Life)
Mr. Michael Novak (American Enterprise Institute)
Fr. Edward Oakes, S.J. (Regis University)
Fr. Thomas P. Rausch, S.J. (Loyola Marymount University)
Mr. George Weigel (Ethics and Public Policy Center)
Dr. Robert Louis Wilken (University of Virginia)

BIBLIOGRAPHY

Abbe de Beaufort. "Practicing the Presence of God." *Decision* (February 1969): 7,13.

"AN AFFIRMATION: Designed to safeguard the unity and liberty of the Presbyterian Church in the United States of America." Reprinted in *The Presbyterian* XCIV (January 17, 1924): 6-7.

Aldrich, Willard M.., "Perseverance." *Bibliotheca Sacra* (115:457; Jan 1958): 9-19.

"An Evangelical Perspective of Roman Catholicism." *Evangelical Review of Theology* (October 1986): 342-364.

Armstrong , John H, ed. The Coming Evangelical Crisis. Chicago: Moody Press, 1996.

Atallah, Ramez L. "Some Trends in the Roman Catholic Church Today." In Let the Earth Hear His Voice. Ed. J. D. Douglas. Minneapolis: World Wide Publications, 1975.

Baille, J. Baptism and Conversion. London: n.p., 1964.

Beale, David O. In Pursuit of Purity. Greenville, SC: Unusual Publications, 1986.

Bosch, David J. "The Church in Dialogue: From Self-Delusion to Vulnerability." In *Missiology: An International Review* (April 1988): 131-145.

"Catholics Laud 'Dr.Graham.' " *Christianity Today* (December 8, 1967): 41-42.

Chafer, Lewis Sperry. Systematic Theology. Grand Rapids: Kregel Publications, 1993.

Chapman, Colin. "Going Soft on Islam." *Vox Evangelica*, (1989): 7-31.

Colson, Chuck. The Body. Dallas: Word Publishing, 1992.

_____ and Richard John Neuhaus, eds. Evangelicals & Catholics Together: Toward a Common Mission. Dallas: Word Publishing, 1995.

_____. "Why Catholics Are Our Allies." *Christianity Today* (November 14, 1994): 136.

Conley , Peter V. "Catholics and the Billy Graham Hub Crusade." *The Pilot* (May 11, 1982).

Corwin, Gary. "House United or Unequal Yoke?" *Evangelical Quarterly Missions* (July 1995): 276-277.

Covell, Ralph R. "The Christian Gospel and World Religions: How much Have American Evangelicals Changed?" *International Bulletin of Missionary Research* (January 1991): 12-16.

Crockett, William V. and James G. Sigountos, Eds. Through No Fault of their Own? Grand Rapids: Baker Book House, 1991.

Davids, Peter H. NICNT: The First Epistle of Peter. Grand Rapids: W. B. Eerdmans Publishing Company, 1990.

Douglas, J. D., ed. Let The Earth Hear His Voice International Congress on World Evangelization, Lauzanne , Switzerland. Minneapolis: World Wide Publications, 1975.

_____. ed. Proclaim Christ Until He Comes International Congress on World Evangelization Lausanne II in Manila. Minneapolis: World Wide Publications, 1990.

Dullea, Carolo W. W. F. 'Billy' Graham's 'Decision for Christ,' A Study in Conversion. Rome: Typis Pontificiae Universitatis Gregorianae, 1971.

Editorial, "Is Evangelical Theology Changing." *Christian Life* (March, 1956): 13-16.

Engelsviken, Tormod. "Ecumenical or evangelical—is there any difference." *Themelios* (Jan/Feb. 1991): 10-13.

Erickson, Millard J. "The Fate of Those Who Never Hear." *Bibliotheca Sacra* (January-March 1995): 3-15.

_____. "Hope for Those Who Have Never Heard? Yes, But..." *Evangelical Missions Quarterly* (April 1975): 122-25.

"Evangelicals & Catholics Together: The Christian Mission in the Third Millennium." *First Things* (May 1994): 15-22.

"Evangelical-Catholic pact questioned." *Christian Century* (March 15,1995): 287.

Ewin, Wilson. "Congress 85: Tragedy in New England." *Baptist Bulletin* (May 1985): 11-12, 33.

Fosdick, Harry Emerson. "Shall the Fundamentalists Win?" Sermon reprint in *Christian Work* CXII (June 10, 1922): 716-22.

Fournier, Keith. Evangelical Catholics. Nashville: Thomas Nelson Publishers, 1990.

Frame, Randy. "Evangelicals, Catholics Pursue New Cooperation." *Christianity Today* (May 16, 1994): 53.

"Fundamentalism and Modernism: Two Religions." Editorial in the *Christian Century*, XL. (January 2, 1994): 5-6.

Geisler, Norman L. "The Concept of Truth in the Inerrancy Debate." *Bibliotheca Sacra* (Vol. 137, No. 548; Oct. 1980): 327-339.

George, Timothy. Ed. "Catholics and Evangelicals in the Trenches." *Christianity Today* (May 16, 1994): 16-17.

George, Timothy. "Evangelicals and Catholics Together: A New Initiative." *Christianity Today* (December 8, 1997): 34.

Graham, Billy. A Biblical Standard for Evangelists. Minneapolis: World Wide Publications, 1984.

_____. "Christian Conversion." *Decision* (November, 1969): 1ff.

_____. "Conversion Personal Revolution." *The Ecumenical Review* (July, 1967): 271-284.

_____. "Loneliness." Personal recording at the Twin Cities Billy Graham Crusade of 1996 (June 19, 1996).

_____. "What Ten Years Have Taught Me." *The Christian Century* (February 17, 1960): 187-188.

Goodchild, Frank M. "Dr. Fosdick's 'Modern Use of the Bible.' " *Watchman Examiner* (February 19, 1925): 235-237.

Greer, Collin. " 'Our Task Is To Do All We Can—Not To Sit And Wait.' " *Parade Magazine* (October 20, 1996): 4-6.

Gregory, H. William. Faith before Faithfulness: Centering the Inclusive Church. Cleveland, OH: Pilgrim Press, 1992.

Houston, Tom. "Let's Stay Together." *World Evangelism* (November-December 1989/January 1990): 8.

Hunter, James Davison. Evangelicalism: The Coming Generation. Chicago: The University of Chicago Press, 1987.

Janssen, Al and Larry K. Weeken, Eds. Seven Promises of a Promise Keeper. Colorado Springs, CO: Focus on the Family Publishing, 1994.

Julianel, Lewis J. The Evil results of the inclusive policy in the Northern Baptist Convention. Chicago: Conservative Baptist Fellowship of Northern Baptists [n.d.].

Kantzer, Kenneth. "Pastoral Letters and the Realities of Life." *Christianity Today* (March 1, 1985): 12.

_____."Should Roman Catholics and Evangelicals Join Ranks?" *Christianity Today* (July 18, 1994): 17.

Lake, Kirsopp. The Religion of Yesterday and Tomorrow. Boston: Houghton Mifflin, 1925.

Lane, Tony. "Evangelicalism and Roman Catholicism." *Evangelical Quarterly* (October 1989): 351-364.

Laws, Curtis Lee. "Are Modernists Christians?" Editorial note in the *Watchman Examiner* (January 7, 1926): 7.

_____. "Convention Sidelights" *Watchman Examiner* (June 7, 1923): 706.

Lenski, R. C. H. "Titus." In The Interpretation of St. Paul's Epistles: Colossians - Philemon. Minneapolis: Augsburg Publishing House, 1964.

Lightner, Robert P. "A Biblical Perspective on False Doctrine." *Bibliotheca Sacra* (January 1985): 16-22.

Lindsell, Harold. The Bible in the Balance. Grand Rapids: Zondervan Publishing House, 1979.

MacArthur, John F. Reckless Faith . Wheaton, IL: Crossway Books, 1994.

Machen, J. Gresham. Christianity and Liberalism. Grand Rapids: Wm. B. Eerdmans Publishing Co, 1946.

"The Manila Manifesto." *World Evangelism* (Special Congress Report, n.d.): 35.

Maring, Norman. "Conservative But Progressive." In What God hath Wrought. Ed. by Gilbert L. Guffin. Chicago: Judson Press, 1960.

Marsden, George M. Fundamentalism and American Culture. Oxford: Oxford University Press, 1980.

Martin, William. A Prophet with Honor. New York: William Morrow and Company, Inc., 1991.

Mattingly, Terri. "Catholics counselors help brethren heed Graham call." *Rocky Mountain News*, Denver, CO. July 7, 1987.

McGrath, Alister. "Do We Still Need the Reformation." *Christianity Today* (December 12, 1994): 28-33.

Meeking, B. and J. Stott, Eds. The Evangelical-Roman Catholic Dialogue on Mission, 1977-1984. A report. Exeter: Paternoster, 1986.

Moran, Bob. "Crusade won't raid Catholic flock, Paulist says." *The Catholic Times* (April 1990): 11.

Morris, Leon. "Hebrews." In the Expositor's Bible Commentary. Ed. Frank E. Gaebelein. Vol. 12. Grand Rapids: Zondervan Publishing House, 1981.

Murray, J. "Repentance" in New Bible Dictionary. Ed. J.D. Douglas. Grand Rapids: Wm. B. Eerdmans Publishing Co., 1962. 1083-1084.

Neuhaus, Richard John. "Nobody Said it Would Be Easy." *First Things* (May 1995): 78-79.

_____. "Protestant Reformation and Universal Church." *First Things* (March 1995): 70.

_____. "A Sense of Change Both Ominous and Promising" *First Things* (August/September 1995): 67-68.

Nicholls, Bruce. "The Salvation and Lostness of Mankind." *Evangelical Review of Theology* (January 1991): 4-21.

Osburn, Evert D. "Those who Have Never Heard: Have they No Hope." *Evangelical Review of Theology* (January 1991): 44-50.

_____. "Those who have never heard, Have They Hope?" *Jets* (September 1989): 367-372

Packer, J. I. "Crosscurrents among Evangelicals." In Evangelicals & Catholics Together: Toward a Common Mission. Ed. by Charles Colson and Richard John Neuhaus. Dallas: Word Publishing, 1995.

_____. "Why I Signed It." *Christianity Today* (December 12, 1994): 34-37

Paisley, Ian R. K. Billy Graham and the Church of Rome. Greenville, SC: Bob Jones University Press, 1970.

Peters, George W. "Perspectives on the Church's Mission. Part IV: Missions in a Religiously Pluralistic World." *Bibliotheca Sacra* (October-December 1979): 291-301.

Pettegrew, Larry D. "Liberation Theology and Hermeneutical Preunderstandings." *Bibliotheca Sacra* (148:591; Jul 1991): 274-87

Phillips, W. Gary. "Evangelical Pluralism: A Singular Problem." *Bibliotheca Sacra* (April-June 1994): 140-54.

Pickering, Ernest D. Promise Keepers and the Forgotten Promise. [pamphlet]. Decatur, AL: Baptist World Mission, n.d.

Pierard, Richard V. "From Evangelical Exclusivism to Ecumenical Openness: Billy Graham and Sociopolitical Issues." *Journal of Ecumenical Studies* (Summer 1983): 425-446.

Pinnock, Clark H. A Wideness in God's Mercy. Grand Rapids: Zondervan Publishing House, 1992.

Pollock, John. Billy Graham: Evangelist to the World. Minneapolis: World Wide Publications, 1979.

Pope John Paul II. A Millennial Hope? Crossing the Threshold of Hope. Ed. Vittorio Messori New York: Knopf, 1994.

Price, Oliver. "Historical Background of the Five Fundamentals." *Bibliotheca Sacra* (January, 1961): 35-40.

Roberts, Alexander and James Donaldson, Eds. The Ante-Nicene Fathers. Vol. V. Grand Rapids: Wm. B. Eerdmans Publishing Company, 1951.

Reapsome, Jim. "What China Doesn't Need." *Christianity Today* (May 16, 1994): 17.

Richard, Ramesh P. The Population of Heaven - A Biblical Response to the inclusivist position on who will be saved. Chicago: Moody Press, 1994.

_____. "Soteriological Inclusivism and Dispensationalism." *Bibliotheca Sacra* (January-March 1994): 85-108.

Quirk, Charles E. "Origins of the Auburn Affirmation." *Journal of Presbyterian History* LIII (Summer, 1975): 120-142.

"The Salvation of the Gentiles— Implication for Other Faiths." *Evangelical Review of Theology.* (January 1991): 36-43.

Sandeen, Ernest R. The Roots of Fundamentalism. Grand Rapids: Baker Book House, 1978. Reprint from University of Chicago, 1970.

Saunders, John. No Other Name. Grand Rapids: William B. Eerdmans Publishing Company, 1992.

Schreck, Alan. Catholic and Christian. Ann Arbor, MI: Servant Books, 1984.

Sproul, R. C. Faith Alone. Grand Rapids: Baker Books, 1995.

Stackhouse, John G. "Billy Graham and the nature of conversion: A paradigm case." *Studies in Religion/Sciences Religieuses* (1992): 337-50.

Stapert, John. "An Ecumenical Spring." *Perspectives* (April 1991): 3.

Tapia, Andrés. "Is a Global Great Awakening Just Around the Corner." *Christianity Today* (November 14, 1994): 80.

Traver, J. H. "The Biology of Salvation" *Bibliotheca Sacra* (July 1963): 251-258.

Trouten, Doug, "Graham comes to Metrodome." In the *Minnesota Christian Chronicle*: Greater Twin Cities Billy Graham Crusade Edition [1996], 1-2.

Tulga, Chester Earl. The Story of the inclusive policy of American Baptist Foreign Mission Society, 1923-1944; a study of theological deception. Chicago: Conservative Baptist Fellowship of Northern Baptists [194?]

Van Gilder, H. O., Ed. "The Irrefutable Logic of the Inclusive Policy." *Baptist Bulletin* (May 1946): 1.

Vencer, Agustin B. Jr. "An International Perspective on Evangelical-Catholic Cooperation." *Evangelical Missions Quarterly* (July 1995): 278-279.

Watchman-Examiner (June 12, 1924): 749.

Zehr, Howard. "Peril Swelling Ranks of Sudanese Christians." *Christianity Today* (April 4, 1994): 80-81.

SCRIPTURE INDEX

GENERAL INDEX

For orders in the USA, please contact:
    Dr. Lance T. Ketchum
    Executive Secretary
    Minnesota Baptist Association
    5000 Golden Valley Road
    Golden Valley, MN 55422
    (763) 588-2755
    Email : order@ebpa-publications.org

For orders in Canada (and other countries):
    Études Bibliques pour Aujourd'hui
    2650 Mont-Joli
    Ste-Foy, PQ G1V-1C6   Canada
    (418) 652 0089
    Email : order@ebpa-publications.org
    visit our website:
    www.ebpa-publications.org

About the author: Raymond L. Teachout is a BWM missionary pastor-
teacher serving with his wife Jennifer in Québec, Canada. He earned his
Bachelors at Northland Baptist Bible College, Dunbar, WI, and his Master
of Divinity at Central Baptist Theological Seminary, Plymouth, MN.
    Contact the author at: jenray@teachouts.org
    Visit their website at: www.teachouts.org/ray&jen